TECHNISCHE UNIVERSITÄT MÜNCHE

Lehrstuhl für Dienstleistungs- und Technologiem

Hedonic Tariff Choice and Consequences of Flat-Rate Bias

The Impact of Consumption Goals on Flat-Rate Bias, and the Competitive Position of a Service Provider as Moderator of Flat-Rate Bias Consequences

- Fabian Uhrich -

Vollständiger Abdruck der von der Fakultät für Wirtschaftswissenschaften der Technischen Universität München zur Erlangung des akademischen Grades eines Doktors der Wirtschaftswissenschaften (Dr. rer. pol.) genehmigten Dissertation.

Vorsitzende:	Univ.-Prof. Dr. Alwine Mohnen
Prüfer der Dissertation:	1. Univ.-Prof. Dr. Florian von Wangenheim
	2. Univ.-Prof. Dr. Helmut Krcmar

Die Dissertation wurde am 12.01.2012 bei der Technischen Universität München eingereicht und durch die Fakultät für Wirtschaftswissenschaften am 15.09.2012 angenommen.

Fabian Uhrich

HEDONIC TARIFF CHOICE AND CONSEQUENCES OF FLAT-RATE BIAS

The Impact of Consumption Goals on Flat-Rate Bias, and the Competitive Position of a Service Provider as Moderator of Flat-Rate Bias Consequences

ibidem-Verlag
Stuttgart

Bibliografische Information der Deutschen Nationalbibliothek
Die Deutsche Nationalbibliothek verzeichnet diese Publikation in der Deutschen Nationalbibliografie; detaillierte bibliografische Daten sind im Internet über http://dnb.d-nb.de abrufbar.

Bibliographic information published by the Deutsche Nationalbibliothek
Die Deutsche Nationalbibliothek lists this publication in the Deutsche Nationalbibliografie; detailed bibliographic data are available in the Internet at http://dnb.d-nb.de.

∞

Gedruckt auf alterungsbeständigem, säurefreien Papier
Printed on acid-free paper

ISBN-13: 978-3-8382-0479-6

Printed in Germany

Deutsche Zusammenfassung

Flat-Rates werden immer populärer. Gleichzeitig tritt auch das Phänomen Flat-Rate Bias immer häufiger auf. Es beschreibt, dass Kunden eine Flat-Rate wählen, obwohl ein nutzungsabhängiger Tarif günstiger für sie wäre. Obwohl der Anteil von Flat-Rate Bias Kunden in verschiedenen Studien stark schwankt, hat bisher noch keine Studie dienstleistungsspezifische Faktoren untersucht, die das Auftreten von Flat-Rate Bias beeinflussen. In fünf Studien zeigt diese Dissertation mit unterschiedlichen Ansätzen, dass das Konsumziel, welches eine Dienstleistung erfüllt, großen Einfluss auf die Tarifwahl hat: Hedonistisch motivierter Konsum führt zu signifikant stärkerem Flat-Rate Bias als utilitaristisch motivierter Konsum. Je hedonistischer eine Dienstleistung wahrgenommen wird, desto ausgeprägter sind Taxi-Meter-, Versicherungs-, und Überschätzungseffekt. Eine stärkere utilitaristische Wahrnehmung hingegen hat keinen signifikanten Einfluss auf Flat-Rate Bias. Dienstleistungsanbieter können daher den Anteil ihrer Flat-Rate Bias Kunden durch Steigerung der hedonistischen Wahrnehmung ihrer Leistung erhöhen.

In einem weiteren Schritt werden die Folgen von Flat-Rate Bias auf die Kundentreue in der Dissertation untersucht. Obwohl die bisherige Forschung keine negativen Konsequenzen auf die Kundentreue festgestellt hat, zeigt die aktuelle Untersuchung ein differenzierteres Bild. Eine Kohorten basierte Ereignisanalyse der Abrechnungsdaten von Internetkunden über zwei Jahre ergibt, dass jeder Euro, den Kunden mit Flat-Rate Bias zu viel zahlen, die erwartete Lebenszeit der Kunden um ein Prozent senkt. Als mögliche Erklärung für diese von der bisherigen Forschung abweichenden Ergebnisse wird in der Dissertation die Marktposition des Dienstleistungsanbieters herangezogen. Die Ergebnisse einer experimentellen Untersuchung von Mobilfunkkunden zeigen, dass die Marktposition die Konsequenzen von Flat-Rate Bias moderiert. Während Low-Cost Anbieter lediglich mit einem erhöhten Tarifwechselrisiko konfrontiert sind, müssen Premium Anbieter mit erhöhtem Kündigungsrisiko rechnen.

Manager von Premium Anbietern müssen daher sorgfältig das Verhalten ihrer Flat-Rate Bias Kunden analysieren und gegebenenfalls Flat-Rate Bias Kunden einen Tarifwechsel anbieten. Low-Cost Anbieter hingegen haben keinen Handlungsbedarf und können von den zusätzlichen Umsätzen voll profitieren.

Executive Summary

Flat-rates become more and more popular for services. At the same time, the occurrence of a flat-rate bias also increases, such that many customers choose flat-rates even if pay-per-use would have been less expensive for them. Although the degree of flat-rate bias varies, no study has analyzed service characteristics that might influence its extent. In five studies combining three different approaches, this dissertation shows that consumption goals of a service have substantial impacts on flat-rate choice: Consuming services to attain hedonic gratification leads to a significantly higher flat-rate bias than using services to fulfill utilitarian needs. The more hedonic a service, the higher the taxi-meter, insurance, and overestimation effect. However, more utilitarian value has no significant impact on the flat-rate bias. Thus, by increasing hedonic perceptions of their services, service providers could increase their share of flat-rate contracts.

In a subsequent step, the dissertation investigates the consequences of a flat-rate bias on customer loyalty. Whereas prior research reports no negative impact of flat-rate bias on customer loyalty, this dissertation provides a more differentiated perspective. A survival analysis of two years transactional data of around 21,490 Internet Service Provider customers reveals that flat-rate bias has a negative effect on churn but not on tariff switching. The expected lifetime of a flat-rate bias customer decreases with every overspent Euro by about 1 percent. The relationship between flat-rate bias and the Customer Lifetime Value is inversely U-shaped. Low degrees of flat-rate bias increase the Customer Lifetime Value while high degrees can reverse this effect. The results of an experimental survey among mobile telephony customers explain these discrepancies to prior findings by showing that the competitive position of a service provider moderates the consequences of flat-rate bias. While low-cost service providers only experience increased tariff switching, premium providers are confronted with an increased churn risk.

Managers of premium service providers are therefore advised to carefully evaluate reactions of their flat-rate bias customer base and potentially proactively manage customers with strong flat-rate bias. Low-cost providers, however, are in no need for action and can benefit from flat-rates without the danger of churn. They should leverage the positive impact of service "hedonization" on the flat-rate bias to increase profits.

Table of Contents

List of Abbreviations

AVE	Average Variance Extracted
CFA	Confirmatory Factor Analysis
CFI	Comparative Fit Index
CI	Confidence Interval
CITC	Corrected Item-to-Total Correlation
CLV	Customer Lifetime Value
Df	Degrees of Freedom
DSL	Digital Subscriber Line
EFA	Exploratory Factor Analysis
EV	Explained Variance
FL	Factor Loading
FnF	Friends and Family
FR	Factor Reliability
HED	Hedonic
HYB	Hybrid
IPTV	Internet Protocol Television
IR	Indicator Reliability
ISP	Internet Service Provider
LL	Lower Limit
M	Mean
RMSEA	Root Mean Square Error of Approximation
RN	Research Now
SE	Standard Error
SRW	Standardized Regression Weight
TLI	Tucker Lewis Index
UL	Upper Limit
UT	Utilitarian
WTP	Willingness to Pay

List of Figures

List of Tables

Acknowledgement

This dissertation was only possible due to great support of many. I want to thank my wife Carolin for tolerating the many ups and downs throughout the whole dissertation process, and for continuously supporting me—already by listening and discussing during long walks. I also want to thank my parents Monika and Siegfried who always encouraged me to take up this challenge, and with their educational effort as foundation stone enabled me to solve it.

Most importantly, I want to thank my Professor, Florian von Wangenheim, as well as Prof. Jan Hendrik Schumann for being extremely approachable, responsive, and constructive while continuously challenging me. They were of essential help as advisors and mentors during the whole academic process—from finding a research topic to applying for scholarships to preparing papers for publication to eventually finishing the dissertation. I could not think of any better support!

Many thanks go also to Prof. Helmut Krcmar who agreed to be my second examiner of this thesis; and to Prof. Alwine Mohnen for being the chairperson of my dissertation committee.

My gratefulness also goes to the Fordham University for granting the 2011 doctoral dissertation award in behavioral pricing to me, the "Leonhard Lorenz Stiftung", and the "Förderverein Kurt Fordan für herausragende Begabungen e.V." for their financial support; to three anonymous reviewers and Prof. Kay Lemon, editor of the Journal of Service Research, who contributed a lot to my research with their detailed feedback and comments.

Finally to all colleagues from the Chair of Service and Technology Marketing and friends who helped me challenge my ideas, and pretest and/or complete my various surveys; especially to Felix and Christoph. Last but not least, the "BCG dissertation community" who made this doctoral dissertation project a great time…

Fabian Uhrich

1 Introduction

1.1 Shortcomings of Flat-Rate Bias Research

1.1.1 Research Gap 1 in the Context of Flat-Rate Bias Causes and Existence

Especially in service sectors, flat-rate tariffs appear increasingly popular (Lambrecht, Seim, & Skiera, 2005; Miravete, 2000). Although most common in telecommunications (Howell, 2010), flat-rates can be found in all industries—from all-inclusive vacation resorts to public transportation day passes to music download platforms. For example, www.napster.co.uk, a UK Internet music portal, offers its users either to pay ~£0.50 for every song, or to subscribe to a flat-rate for £5 per month independent of the amount of downloads. For heavy users, unlimited consumption at a fixed price can be a bargain. Yet many customers exhibit a flat-rate bias and choose this pricing scheme even though a pay-per-use tariff would have been less expensive for them. Multiple studies confirm the existence of the bias (e.g., Hobson & Spady, 1988; Kling & van Der Ploeg, 1990; Nunes, 2000). Lambrecht and Skiera (2006) identify four potential causes for it: the convenience effect (having no need for complicated pay-per-use calculations), the taxi-meter effect (when the ticking of the taxi meter lowers the consumption experience of a taxi-ride), the insurance effect (against unexpected losses), and the overestimation effect (i.e. simply wrong demand forecast). Interestingly, the degree of flat-rate bias varies significantly across studies and industries. Mitchell and Vogelsang (1991) report that 45% of households pay too much for telephone packages, and Nunes (2000), in a survey of health club users, finds that 61% overpay. However, for Internet services, Lambrecht and Skiera (2006) identify only 38% of customers who would have saved money with variable pricing. As flat-rate bias directly increases revenues and subsequently profit, understanding these variations is very important for service providers. Knowing what service characteristics drive flat-rate bias helps service providers to make better pricing decisions and finally improve their profits.

Understanding the variance of flat-rate bias across services is also important for researchers. A flat-rate bias contradicts standard economic theory, according to which customers try to maximize their welfare and choose the rate that leads to minimal costs (Khan, Dhar, & Wertenbroch, 2004). Researchers need to understand the conditions in which standard economic theory fails to predict price plan choice. Behavioral decision research deals with such situations (Loewenstein, 2001) by considering consumption goals, such that "consumer choices are driven by utilitarian and hedonic considerations" (Dhar & Wertenbroch, 2000, p. 60). Researchers have demonstrated that consumption goals affect product choice (e.g., Maslow, 1968) and product evaluations (e.g., Okada, 2005); they also likely influence tariff choices and even might help explain differences in the level of flat-rate bias.

If service providers know the impact of consumption goals on tariff choice, they could prime their services respectively to increase customers' bias. The potential impact of consumption goals on tariff choice and thus on flat-rate bias has not been studied previously though.

1.1.2 Research Gap 2 in the Context of Flat-rate Bias Consequences[1]

Although actively increasing flat-rate bias seems great for service providers at first sight as they benefit from constant revenues at a higher level than with pay-per-use, the question is whether this is sustainable in the long-term? If customers become aware of paying too much with their flat-rate, economic theory predicts that they will change to a cheaper alternative (Brown & Sibley, 1986; Khan et al., 2004). This can be achieved either by switching the tariff within the service provider or by churning to a competitor. Service providers must decide whether they should offer these endangered customers another tariff (e.g., pay-per-use) before they potentially churn to a competitor, or whether they do not need to react and can benefit from the higher revenues.

Despite this high managerial relevance, research on this question is still scarce. A first study on the consequences of flat-rate bias on customer behavior (Lambrecht & Skiera, 2006) finds an impact on customer tariff switching but no impact on churn. General research on tariff choice, however, shows that customers who subscribe to the wrong calling plan have lower retention rates than those subscribing to the financially most attractive one (Joo, Jun, & Kim, 2002; Wong, 2010a). This seems plausible as customers who become aware of the wrong tariff choice might not only question their tariff but also their provider to whom they

[1] This chapter is based on joint research with Felix Frank.

potentially attribute this failure (Peterson, Semmel, Baeyer, & Abramson, 1982; Riess, Rosenfeld, Melburg, & Tedeschi, 1981). As the attractiveness of competitive offers is the main driver of customer loyalty (Morgan & Hunt, 1994), customers will churn if they find more attractive, cheaper tariffs in the market. The potential savings by competitive offers are determined by the competitive position of the service provider. Low-cost providers try to offer their services at the lowest price in the market or at least the lowest price to value ratio (Porter, 1980). Thus savings from competitive offers are limited by definition of the market segment. Premium service providers instead focus on differentiation and have rather high prices (Porter, 1980) leaving more space for potential savings from competitors. A differentiation of the consequences of flat-rate bias by the competitive position of the service provider has not been made so far and could resolve the converse findings of Lambrecht and Skiera (2006) with general research on tariff choice (Joo et al., 2002; Wong, 2010a).

1.2 Research Questions and Goal of this Dissertation

This dissertation aims at extending flat-rate bias research in two dimensions—drivers of flat-rate bias effects and thus flat-rate bias variance (research gap 1), and a more differentiated understanding of its consequences by identifying a potential moderator (research gap 2). To fill the first research gap, the dissertation analyzes potential drivers of flat-rate bias causes and subsequently the extent of flat-rate bias. Specifically, it investigates the impact of consumption goals on tariff choice potentially explaining part of the variance of the extent of flat-rate bias among existing research. It addresses the following research question: (RQ_1) Do service consumption goals affect flat-rate bias effects and subsequently flat-rate bias?

To fill the second research gap, the dissertation re-investigates the consequences of flat-rate bias on customer loyalty—namely switching and churn. Existing research on the consequences of flat-rate bias (i.e., no impact on churn) contradicts general tariff choice research (i.e., negative impact of suboptimal tariff choice on customer loyalty). To solve these converse findings, this dissertation poses the following research questions: (RQ_2) Does flat-rate bias increase tariff switching and customer churn? And (RQ_3) does the competitive position of a service provider moderate flat-rate bias consequences?

For practitioners this dissertation shall provide a tool to actively manage the extent of flat-rate bias of service customers by manipulating consumption goals while maintaining the sustainability of the Customer Lifetime Value (CLV) by taking the consequences of flat-rate bias on customer loyalty into account. For researchers, the findings shall help explain existing variances of the extent of flat-rate bias among studies, and resolve the converse findings regarding the impact of flat-rate bias on customer loyalty between the study by Lambrecht and Skiera (2006) and general tariff choice research (Joo et al., 2002; Wong, 2010a).

1.3 Structure of this Dissertation

The remaining part of this dissertation is structured as follows: Chapter 2 provides the relevant research background on flat-rate pricing, flat-rate bias causes in combination with consumption goal theory as a potential driver, and on flat-rate bias consequences including the competitive position as potential moderator. Chapter 3 analyzes the potential impact of consumption goals on flat-rate bias effects and the extent of flat-rate bias closing research gap 1 and answering research question 1. It contains the hypotheses development at the level of the four flat-rate bias effects, a description of the research methodology to test those hypotheses, and the results of the empirical tests including a discussion from a theoretical and a managerial point of view. Chapter 4 investigates the consequences of flat-rate bias on customer loyalty including the impact of the competitive position as a potential moderator closing research gap 2 by answering research questions 2 and 3. It starts with the development of hypotheses based on existing knowledge, followed by a description of the research methodology including a description of the empirical data set, and contains the results from the hypotheses tests including a discussion from a theoretical and a managerial point of view. Chapter 5 summarizes the results of Chapters 3 and 4, and provides theoretical and managerial implications from an overall perspective. Figure 1 shows the structure of this dissertation graphically.

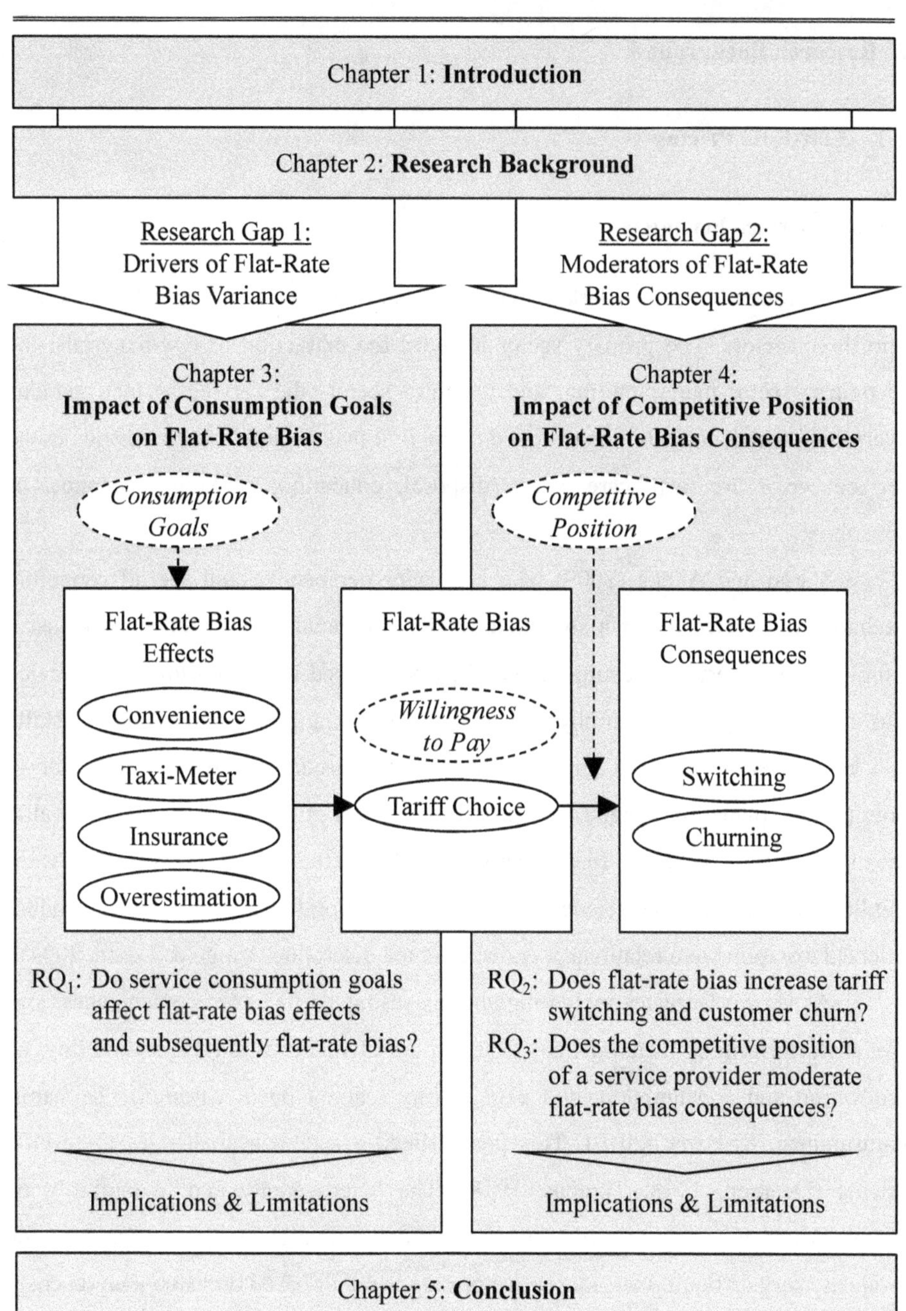

Figure 1—Structure of this Dissertation

2 Research Background

2.1 Flat-Rate Pricing

2.1.1 Service Pricing

Historically, Colin Clark and Jean Forastié (Wolfe, 1955) split the economy into three sectors. The primary sector includes the extraction of raw-materials, the secondary sector manufacturing, and the third sector (the service sector) contains everything which could not be assigned to the first two. Examples of industries in the service sector are healthcare, waste disposal, education, banking, insurance, or consulting.

Vargo and Akaka (2009) take a broader perspective and see all economic exchange as service under a so called service dominant logic. Products are just a simple form of service creating value when being used by the customer. A service can include everything from physical products to intangible resources such as skills and know-how. A museum for example combines products (e.g., exhibits), know-how (e.g., explanation panels), and processes (e.g., a guided tour) to achieve value creation at the customer (e.g., learning and entertainment). This has several implications on marketing science developing marketing from a transactional product oriented discipline to a relational, service oriented discipline (Vargo & Lusch, 2004).

As shown, services include intangible resources like core competences, and are characterized by heterogeneity (due to nonstandardization), inseparability of production and consumption, and perishability (cannot be inventoried) (Zeithaml, Parasuraman, & Berry, 2010). This poses specific and new challenges to service pricing (Dearden, 1978; Thomas, 1978). The heterogeneity and intangibility of resources makes a resource cost based price determination, which is common for products, very difficult. Instead, service pricing is rather based on value than on costs (Thomas, 1978). This implies the risk that low service prices induce a perceived low service quality (Thomas, 1978). Furthermore, the inseparability of production and consumption together with the perishability of services poses specific challenges for pricing to best match offer and demand. Yield management, balancing demand in order to best utilize the perishable capacity, therefore is an important function (Desiraju & Shugan, 1999). In the telecommunications industry for example this means to avoid unused, lost capacity during times of low usage while ensuring that during usage peaks capacity constraints are not exceeded. Price differentiation by usage time or service level (e.g., connection speed or quality) is one means of yield management to optimizing service capacity. This leaves the customer in charge of choosing "the right" tariff from a menu of different price plans. Besides optimizing capacity usage, price differentiation and tariffs are also a means to skim customers' willingness to pay and optimize profits for service providers.

2.1.2 Price Differentiation

In economics, demand curves describe the relationship between prices and demanded quantity (Figure 2).

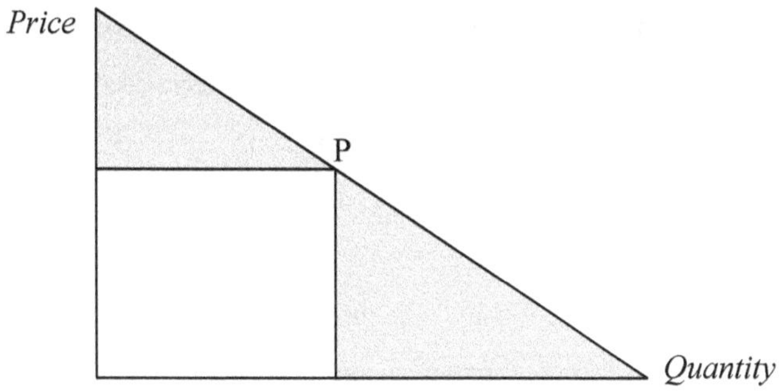

Figure 2—Illustrative Demand Curve

If service providers offer their service for only one price to the market, they face two disadvantages. First, they miss part of the customers who cannot afford the service at this price (triangle at the lower right). Second, they sell their services to other customers who would have paid much more (upper left triangle). To solve these disadvantages, companies try to differentiate their prices and skim the so called consumer surplus. Price differentiation is a very common method in marketing and used since very long time. Pigou (1920) differentiates three types of price discrimination.

First-degree or "perfect" price discrimination means that a company sells its services to every customer at a different price depending on his or her individual willingness to pay. This leads to the maximum profit of the service provider but is very hard to implement in real life. Companies must minimize or eliminate the risk that customers with a high willingness to pay get the service for a lower price. Examples of successful first-degree price discrimination in practice are individualized contracts of automotive suppliers or auction pricing where customers indicate their willingness to pay with the maximum price they offer in the bidding process.

Second-degree price discrimination means that all customers who consume the same amount of a service pay the same price. Thus the price depends on the volume and not the consumer. Typical examples are volume discounts such as time packages for telecommunications or flat-rate tariffs.

Third-degree price discrimination happens if providers sell the same volume to different people for different prices. A typical example here is a student discount where the price depends on the customer group and not the amount.

Second- and third-degree price discrimination is much easier to implement in practice than first-degree price discrimination. The criteria determining the price per customer are transparent and can be shown easily in a price list. Furthermore, customers can not get the wrong price as the criteria are easy to check and objectively measurable. Thus service providers in practice try to leverage second and third degree price discrimination by offering a menu of different tariffs. Customers then can choose the right one for them according to their needs and characteristics maximizing the consumer surplus for the provider along the demand curve.

2.1.3 Typical Tariff Types

Typical tariffs under second-degree price discrimination can be classified as either one-, two-, or three-part tariffs depending on how many central pricing elements they contain (Lambrecht et al., 2005). One-part tariffs only contain one pricing element. The most typical linear one-part tariff is pay-per-use. Under a pay-per-use tariff, customers have to pay a specific amount of money for every unit they consume. This unit can be for example time, volume, or rides. The more consumers use a service the more they pay for it. If they do not use the service at all they are not getting charged anything. A typical example for a one-part pay-per-use tariff is a simple metro ticket. People pay a specific amount of money for every metro ride they do—if they do not use the metro at all they do not pay any money, neither. In contrast to this, flat-rate tariffs are independent of the actual consumption. The customer pays a fixed fee allowing the possibility to consume as much as possible. Monthly passes for the metro system can demonstrate this logic very well. Buying a monthly ticket allows the user to do unlimited metro rides. However, if the user does not use the metro at all during this period, he still pays the full price.

Two-part tariffs charge a fixed access fee plus a variable fee. The fixed fee simply grants access to the service but does not contain any usage. For example, most post-paid mobile phone contracts follow this principle. To get access to the mobile network, users pay a monthly fee. This allows them to receive calls but as soon as they want to call out themselves they have to pay a price per minute for usage.

Three-part tariffs already provide the user a specific amount of usage, before the variable pricing starts (Lambrecht et al., 2005). Mobile data tariffs often use this system. For a monthly fee the user can download data until a certain volume is reached. After this volume, he gets charged a marginal price for every additional Megabyte of usage. Figure 3 provides an overview comparing the three tariff types.

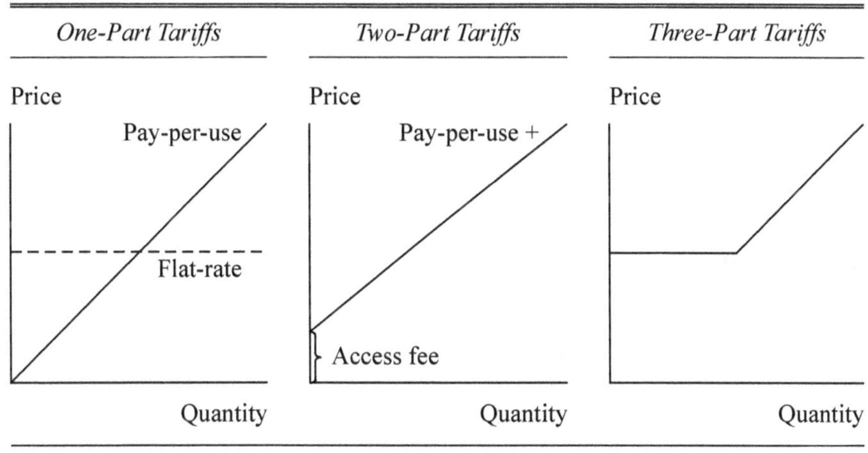

Figure 3—Tariff Types

2.1.4 Flat-Rate Pricing in the Service Sector

Flat-rates are a key pricing structure in today's price menus of service providers and appear increasingly popular (Lambrecht et al., 2005; Miravete, 2000). Although most common in telecommunications, flat-rates can be found in all industries—from all-inclusive vacation resorts to public transportation day passes to music download platforms. Table 1 lists all service classes defined by the German industry sector code (Statistisches Bundesamt, 2009) and shows some examples of flat-rate tariffs.

Code	*Name*	*Selected Flat-Rate Examples*
D	Utilities: energy	Furnished housing including fixed fee for energy usage
E	Utilities: water, waste mgmt.	Fixed fee for household waste disposal independent of the actual amount of waste produced
F	Construction	Turn-key houses
G	Car retail/repairs	Mobility guarantee for cars (includes all repair costs)
H	Traffic, storage	Day-passes or monthly tickets for public transportation
I	Gastronomy	All-you-can eat buffets
J	Information and communication	Music/video flat-rates, newspaper subscriptions, telephony/internet flat-rates, scientific journals database
K	Insurance	Health insurance, flat-rate for glasses / contact lenses
L	Real estate	No example
M	Scientific and technical services	Fixed fee consulting contracts
N	Other business services	Fixed fee car rental independent of driven kilometers
O	Public admin.	No example
P	Education	Fixed price for MBA program independent of classes
Q	Health & social	No example
R	Arts & entertain.	Museum / amusement park day passes, sports clubs
S	Other services	No example

Table 1—Examples of Flat-Rate Services by Industry Sector Code

2.2 Flat-Rate Bias Causes and Consumption Goals

2.2.1 Flat-Rate Bias Causes

2.2.1.1 Existence of Flat-Rate Bias

When making service decisions, customers usually have to choose among several offered tariffs, such as pay-per-use or flat-rate options. As customers often decide under uncertainty about their future usage, they sometimes make economically suboptimal choices (Lambrecht et al., 2005). For example, many customers exhibit a flat-rate bias and choose this pricing scheme even though a pay-per-use tariff would have been less expensive for them. Train (1991, p. 211) already defines flat-rate bias as a situation in which consumers "value flat-rate service over measured service even when the bill that the consumer would receive under the two services … would be the same". The use and understanding of flat-rate bias in this dissertation follows this definition. Many research studies confirm its existence in various contexts (see Table 2).

Authors	*Data Set*	*Key Results*
Existence of flat-rate bias in usage data		
Train, McFadden, & Ben-Akiva, 1987	Telephone usage data of 2,963 households	Existence of flat-rate bias
Hobson & Spady, 1988	Telephone usage data of 172 households	Existence of flat-rate bias
Train, Ben-Akiva, & Atherton, 1989	Telephone usage data of 520 households	Existence of flat-rate bias
Kling & van Der Ploeg, 1990	Telephone usage data of 1,456 households	Existence of flat-rate bias
Degree of flat-rate bias in usage data		
Mitchell & Vogelsang, 1991	Telephone usage data of 151,000 households	Consumers without usage chose packages; 45% of flat-rate customers pay too much
Kridel et al., 1993	Telephone usage data of 2,786 households	76% of flat-rate customers pay too much
Nunes, 2000	Survey among 129 health club users	61% of flat-rate customers pay too much: → savings with pay-per-use: ~38% / $230 p.a.
Miravete, 2002	Usage data of 1,542 telephone households	6–12% of flat-rate customers pay too much: → savings with pay-per-use: ~22% / $72 p.a.
Della Vigna & Malmendier, 2006	Gym usage data of 7,978 customers	80% of monthly fee customers pay too much: → savings with pay-per-use: ~40% / $500
Lambrecht & Skiera, 2006	Usage data of 10,882 Internet service provider customers	38% of flat-rate customers pay too much: → savings with pay-per-use: ~50% (for 50% of flat-rate bias customers)
Flat-rate bias in tariff choice experiments		
Prelec & Loewenstein, 1998	Survey among 89 airport visitors for four services	52% of respondents prefer flat-rate
Nunes, 2000	Survey among 120 students regarding a swimming pool	35-93% of respondents prefer flat-rates
Nunes, 2000	Survey among 100 grocery shoppers regarding an online supermarket	87% of respondents prefer flat-rate
Lambrecht & Skiera, 2006	Survey among 241 students	18–95% of respondents prefer flat-rate (at same price level)

Table 2—Flat-Rate Bias Literature Overview

The degree of flat-rate bias significantly varies across studies and industries. Mitchell and Vogelsang (1991) report that 45% of households pay too much for telephone packages, and Nunes (2000), in a survey of health club users, finds that 61% overpay. However, for Internet services, Lambrecht and Skiera (2006) identify only 38% of customers who would have saved money with variable pricing. Despite those significant differences regarding the extent of flat-rate bias, no research has analyzed service characteristics that might influence its extent.

Lambrecht and Skiera (2006) cluster the causes of flat-rate bias into four effects: the convenience, taxi-meter, insurance, and overestimation effect. In the following chapters, the four effects get explained individually and in detail.

2.2.1.2 Convenience Effect

A convenience effect occurs when the consumer chooses a flat-rate tariff to avoid the need for pay-per-use calculations. Especially when many alternatives are available, customers likely make the "easiest" choice, whether that means the most common tariff, a promoted tariff, or the one with the easiest structure.

The convenience effect can be explained by transaction cost theory (Nunes, 2000). Deciding for a tariff generates internal and external search cost (Smith, Venkatraman, & Dholakia, 1999). External search costs for example include the opportunity costs of the time needed to gather information about tariffs. This gets especially relevant if people are used to a tariff. Choosing the same tariff saves the external search costs of gathering information about other tariffs. This applies to both, tariff switching as well as the choice of a new tariff.

Internal search costs cover the mental effort of understanding the tariff structure, determining the projected costs based on the assumed usage behavior, and comparing the projected costs of potential tariffs. If the tariff structure is complex, customers need to exert effort to estimate their expected usage and calculate the respective costs (Winer, 2005). Compared to pay-per-use tariffs, flat-rate plans are easy to understand (one price independent of the usage), and the costs are well known in advance lowering the internal search costs.

Besides those upfront costs, also the costs of handling the payments can be different between pay-per-use and flat-rate tariffs. In non-contractual settings, payments are often manual, so pay-per-use customers have more effort to pay, such as buying a ticket for every train ride. A flat-rate eliminates this repeated effort and increases convenience, such that the consumer only needs to buy a monthly ticket every 30 days. With increasing pervasiveness of electronic payment systems, this difference may get lost. For example, to use public transportation in Hong Kong, a chip card gains access to the trains for every ride. This procedure is independent from the chosen tariff, be it flat-rate or pay-per-use, and so handling costs are also equal in both cases. The same applies to contractual settings, where payments are handled automatically by direct debiting or credit cards.

Kling and van Der Ploeg (1990) were the first to measure a convenience effect based on a scale reflecting the inertia to change habits. Lambrecht and Skiera (2006) instead did not find a significant impact of the convenience effect on flat-rate bias. To better understand its impact, this dissertation includes the convenience effect as a potential cause of flat-rate bias and will add empirical evidence regarding its influence to the research body of flat-rate bias.

2.2.1.3 Taxi-Meter Effect

A taxi-meter effect arises when consumers do not want to "hear" the price ticking upward as they use the service. It reminds them of the pain of paying and lowers their consumption enjoyment (Lambrecht & Skiera, 2006).

The theory underlying the taxi-meter effect is mental accounting (Heath & Soll, 1996; Kivetz, 1999; Shefrin & Thaler, 1992; Thaler, 1985) and is based on prospect theory (Kahneman & Tversky, 1979). Mental accounting assumes an implicit accounting system, with virtual budgets and accounts for consumption (Thaler, 1985). A purchase decision causes the consumer to open a mental account that contains all related benefits and costs. Users enjoy the benefits from consumption, but the costs constitute pain that lowers their pleasure (Prelec & Loewenstein, 1998). The evaluation of benefits and costs can be done separately and jointly. High losses combined with low gains are called "mixed losses". The higher the losses in such a context, the more likely consumers tend to segregate the losses from the gains. This would mean that they use the relatively small gains to compensate and console themselves for the losses. For multiple gains consumers also prefer segregation as several low gains are valued higher than a single gain with the cumulative value. In contrast, multiple losses get preferably integrated to reduce the moments of pain. Credit cards follow this logic and integrate several losses into one. The same applies for mixed gains, this means gains and losses with a higher share of gains, where consumers prefer integration to hide the losses under the gains. The overall benefit from service consumption then is the sum of all benefits minus all costs and pains in the account evaluated separately or jointly over time.

If a payment occurs in advance (or can be mentally depreciated by assigning it to the flat-rate), users can forget the pain of payment while they consume and enjoy the service (Lambrecht & Skiera, 2006; Nunes, 2000). Therefore, users generally have a preference for prepayment (Prelec & Loewenstein, 1998). The pain of paying gets eased by thoughts about the benefits of consumption in the future at the moment of payment. While consumption in the future can be enjoyed as if it were free as there are no more marginal costs. In contrast, a pay-per-use tariff forces consumers to think about costs constantly, which lowers their perceived benefits (Kivetz, 1999).

All-inclusive holidays are a good example to understand the logic of the taxi-meter effect. Once the vacations are paid in advance, eating, drinking, and sleeping can be enjoyed without any thoughts about the costs. Although factored into the price already, consumers perceive the services free of charge. Conversely, they had to pay every single drink which would lower their fun and enjoyment of consumption, even if the total cost would be the same.

The first to show a relationship between enjoyment and flat-rate pricing were Prelec and Loewenstein (1998). In a survey on an airport they asked 89 subjects about the enjoyment of a third person using different services under pay-per-use versus flat-rate pricing. In three of four services (food during dine cruise, health club, long distance phone calls) the majority thought that enjoyment is larger under fixed pricing. Only for the case of public transportation there was no clear result. Lambrecht and Skiera (2006) developed a detailed measurement scale for the taxi-meter effect and were able to show a significant impact of the effect on flat-rate bias.

2.2.1.4 Insurance Effect

An insurance effect happens if customers want to anticipate the risk of over-usage or demand variability, which could cause financial losses. Therefore, they give up the opportunity to pay less and instead set a ceiling to avoid paying more. Three theories explain the insurance effect: risk aversion, loss aversion, and option value.

Risk-averse behavior emerges when people prefer a flat-rate because they fear the uncertainty that they might pay more (Miravete, 2000; Nunes, 2000; Train, 1991). Risk-averse customers are willing to pay a premium for a determined outcome even if the expected outcome (weighted by the statistical probability) is higher. An easy example to demonstrate risk-averse behavior is the choice situation between the following two options: playing the lottery to gain €100 with a 50:50 chance versus a fixed gain of €40. In the first situation, the expected utility would be €50 whereas the second choice yields €40 only. Risk-averse customers prefer the €40 gain, as they do not want to face the risk to gain nothing. Applied to tariff choice situations, risk-averse customers prefer a fixed monthly fee over variable pricing giving up the opportunity to pay less in order to exclude the risk of paying more.

An explanation for this behavior is loss aversion. As part of prospect theory, it means that a loss evokes stronger negative feelings than the same amount of gain evokes positive feelings (Kahneman & Tversky, 1979; Tversky & Kahneman, 1991). In contrast to utility theory that evaluates choices based on an expected overall value (e.g., the expected value weighted by its probability), prospect theory evaluates delta changes (gains and losses) to a reference point of a status quo. Gains and losses thereby show different value functions—concave for gains, and convex for losses. The loss curves further have a steeper slope than the gain curves (see Figure 4).

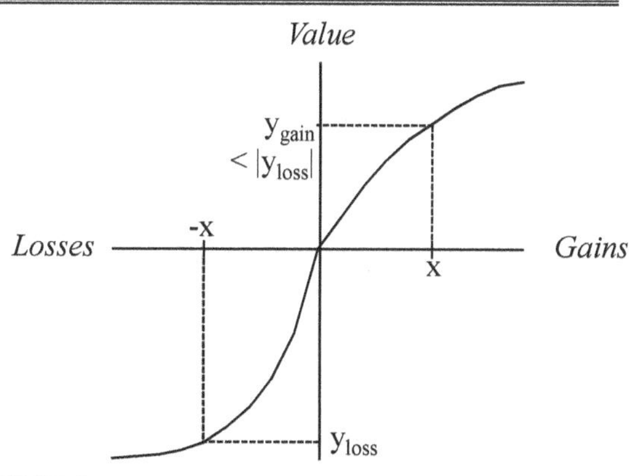

Figure 4—Illustrative Value Function of Gains and Losses (Kahneman & Tversky, 1979)

Thus, the loss of €10 would be perceived as more negative than the gain of €10. Applied to tariff choice this means that with pay-per-use pricing, the bill amount disperses around an expected value, with interim losses and gains balancing over the long term. For loss-averse customers, the negative feelings of losses outweigh the positive feelings of gains though, so they prefer a constant bill to varying interim losses and gains (Lambrecht & Skiera, 2006).

Finally, the option value of a flat-rate describes the possibility that the customer will consume more than originally planned at the same price. In literature, an option value describes "the value of an option to use a resource (or service) in an uncertain world, where the uncertainty can involve preferences, income, prices, and/or supply" (Kridel et al., 1993, p. 129f). In pricing, the option value gets directly addressed by emerging car or bike sharing services. In Germany, users must pay a registration fee to get access to the sharing system. This access fee on the provider side covers administrative costs, and on the customer side is the value of the option to use bike or car sharing in the future. In the context of tariff choice, the option value of a flat-rate is the possibility to use the service more often in the future even if currently pay-per-use might be the cheaper choice.

Empirically, the insurance effect has been proven to be a strong cause of flat-rate bias by several researchers already (e.g., Lambrecht & Skiera, 2006; Train et al., 1989). Kridel, Lehman, and Weisman (1993), for example, find an option value of $9.5 for flat-rates—however, this only covers one facet of the insurance effect.

2.2.1.5 Overestimation Effect

Overestimation occurs when customers overestimate their expected usage. Several factors foster overestimation. Advertisement for instance can make customers think to use a service more than they actually will do (Mitchell & Vogelsang, 1991). Showing vignettes of intense service usage suggests customers that they will also use the service that intensely. Also the type of presentation can make the service more desirable.

Thus, customers might fall for wishful thinking (Einhorn & Hogarth, 1986), another explanation of the overestimation effect (Nunes, 2000). Even if customers do not use the service enough today to justify a flat-rate, they may simply want themselves to use the service more often in the future. Especially if consequences of using the service are desirable, customers commit to a flat-rate in order to force themselves to use the service more intensely (Wertenbroch, 1998). This is a typical phenomenon for health clubs where users are over-confident in their self-control (Della Vigna & Malmendier, 2006).

Often, the overestimation effect is just a result of an inaccurate demand forecast. Parducci's range-frequency model explains the general existence of overestimation bias (Nunes, 2000). Any usage has a natural minimum of zero. The amount of possible outcomes below an expected value is limited, and lower than the amount of possible outcomes above an expected value. Therefore people perceive a higher likelihood to consume more than to consume less. They choose the tariff rather based on this subjective likelihood of over- and under-usage than on the expected average usage.

Nunes (2000) showed in his study how varying minimum and maximum historic usage ranges influence decision making. He called this procedure ratio-rule. Following it, flat-rate bias is driven by the extent to which maximum (q_{max}) and minimum (q_{min}) usage differs from the break-even (q_{be}) amount. The larger the upper range ($q_{max} - q_{be}$) compared to the lower range ($q_{be} - q_{min}$), the more people believe the likelihood of over-usage to be larger than the likelihood of under-usage:

$$Ratio = \frac{q_{max} - q_{be}}{q_{be} - q_{min}}$$

In two experiments he has proven a significant impact of this ratio rule on flat-rate bias. Lambrecht and Skiera (2006) used the ratio rule in their research identifying a significant impact on flat-rate bias. However, a larger variance does not only trigger overestimation based on Paraducci's range-frequency model. It also triggers higher uncertainty which increases the insurance effect. Therefore, the ratio rule is not used as approximation of the overestimation effect in this dissertation. Instead, a multi-item scale gets developed in a later section.

2.2.2 Consumption Goals

2.2.2.1 Behavioral Decision Research

As just seen on the example of flat-rate bias, standard economic theory often fails to fully explain human decision behavior: Instead of choosing the economically more attractive pay-per-use tariff, flat-rate bias customers choose a flat-rate instead. This decision cannot be explained by pure economic theory, "according to which consumers maximize utility in a rational and cognitively driven manner" (Khan et al., 2004, p.1) when making decisions. Only when taking cognitive and emotional factors into account, such behavior becomes comprehensible (Simonson, Carmon, Dhar, Drolet, & Nowlis, 2001). Besides flat-rate bias, also other biases in human information processing like underweighting base rates, overconfidence, hindsight bias, and misperceptions of random sequences cannot be explained by economic theory solely (Loewenstein, 2001). Behavioral decision theory deals with such "failures" of economic theory incorporating concepts of psychology.

Focus areas of behavioral decision research are the processes underlying judgments and decisions, and the resulting phenomena. For example, research has shown (Simonson et al., 2001) that the framing of product attributes (e.g., beef that is "80% lean" versus has "20% fat") influences product evaluation (Levin & Gaeth, 1988); that if costs incur before benefits, sunk cost effects are strongly diminished (Gourville & Soman, 1998); that preference elicitation tasks like comparing several options (e.g., product choice), rating individual options, and matching two options with varying price and quality, result in significantly different preferences (Carmon & Simonson, 1998). Mental accounting (Thaler, 1985) and prospect theory (Kahneman & Tversky, 1979)—the foundation of the taxi-meter and the insurance effect—are also key concepts of behavioral decision research.

2.2.2.2 Consumption Goal Research

Another important concept of behavioral decision research are consumption goals as means to understand customer behavior (Simonson et al., 2001): Consumers use services "for two basic reasons: (1) consummatory affective (hedonic) gratification (from sensory attributes), and (2) instrumental, utilitarian reasons concerned with 'expectations of consequences' (of a means-ends variety, from functional and nonsensory attributes)" (Batra & Ahtola, 1991, p. 159).

Hedonic consumption aims at pleasure, fun, and enjoyment and is related to aesthetic, experiential, and enjoyment-related benefits (Chitturi, Raghunathan, & Mahajan, 2008). Hedonic goods are often seen as luxuries, hedonic services as multisensory. At the extreme, they may be considered even frivolous or decadent (O'Curry & Strahilevitz, 2001). Typical examples of hedonic goods include flowers, sports cars, chocolate, or luxury watches (Khan et al., 2004). Hedonic services are for instance listening to music, going to the movies, or riding a rollercoaster.

Utilitarian consumption instead reflects functional needs and requirements and is related to instrumental and practical benefits (Chitturi et al., 2008). Utilitarian goods and services are practical, instrumental, necessary, or functional (O'Curry & Strahilevitz, 2001). Typical examples of utilitarian goods are microwaves, detergents, or minivans (Khan et al., 2004). Utilitarian services include for instance going to the dentist, visiting a take-out lunch counter, or using tax advisors.

These two consumption goals are not necessarily two ends of a continuum (Voss, Spangenberg, & Grohmann, 2003); services often score high on both dimensions simultaneously (Okada, 2005). Moreover, the evaluation of these dimensions is highly subjective and case dependent. For example, using the telephone to call for help makes it utilitarian; using the service to chat with friends makes it hedonic (Khan et al., 2004).

2.2.2.3 Impact of Consumption Goals on Consumer Behavior

The impact of consumption goals on consumer behavior has been studied extensively under various conditions (Chitturi, Raghunathan, & Mahajan, 2007; Dhar & Wertenbroch, 2000; Khan et al., 2004; Okada, 2005; Voss et al., 2003); from pre-consumption decision behavior to post-consumption consequences:

Chitturi, Raghunathan, and Mahajan (2007), for example, demonstrate that, once a certain level of functionality is reached, consumers pay more attention to the hedonic than to the utilitarian dimension. This is also in line with the concept of the hierarchical pyramid of needs (Maslow, 1968). Lower levels contain mainly necessities that are needed to relieve discomfort (C. J. Berry, 1994), while the higher levels focus on self-realization, and are luxuries leading to comfort and pleasure in life. Similarly, consumers need to earn the right to indulge before they can focus on hedonic consumption goals. Without, they rather prefer the utilitarian dimension (Kivetz & Simonson, 2002).

Preference between hedonic and utilitarian consumption goals also depends on the response-mode (Khan et al., 2004). Hedonic consumption induces feelings of guilt and justification (Okada, 2005). Therefore, utilitarian goods are preferred to hedonic goods in a direct comparison. The negative feelings of guilt to choose a hedonic alternative if a utilitarian alternative was offered drive this effect. When the alternatives are evaluated independent from each other, hedonic alternatives are evaluated higher than utilitarian. Hence, hedonic goods are also more popular if won as prizes, whereas utilitarian are preferred in purchase situations. For one, it may be that uncertain situations make consumers favor hedonic alternatives while certainty makes consumers favor utilitarian (O'Curry & Strahilevitz, 2001). Additionally, winning something as a prize is independent of guilt and justification (due to the payment) which would lower the enjoyment from hedonic consumption. In a similar vein, Strahilevitz and Myers (1998) document that, when tied to charities, preference for hedonic consumption gets improved as the spending on charity compensates for the feelings of guilt. The same applies to rewards gained in frequency programs such as Lufthansa Miles & More where hedonic rewards are preferred to utilitarian (Kivetz & Simonson, 2002).

Also price sensitivity changes depending on the consumption goal. Affect-rich, hedonic consumption evokes an emotional decision mode with evaluation by feeling while affect-poor utilitarian consumption evokes a more rational decision with evaluation by calculation (Hsee & Rottenstreich, 2004; Kahneman, Ritov, & Schkade, 2000). Thus, consuming hedonic services customers are less price sensitive than when consuming utilitarian services (Wakefield & Inman, 2003).

Furthermore, researchers have found out that the reference influences the evaluation of consumption goals. "For example, an apartment with a better view (relatively hedonic feature) is preferred over an apartment with a shorter commute to work (relatively utilitarian feature) when the decision maker's current apartment has both a nice view and a short commute than when the current apartment has neither of the two features. In other words, when people are making a forfeiture decision they are more likely to give up the utilitarian option than the hedonic one" (Khan et al. 2004, p. 9).

Finally, also post-consumption behavior gets affected by the consumption goals. Chitturi, Raghunathna, and Mahajan (2008) show that hedonic consumption can lead to customer delight and subsequently to higher customer satisfaction, word-of-mouth, and repurchase intentions than utilitarian consumption.

As shown, the impact of consumption goals has been analyzed in various studies. An impact of the consumption goals on tariff choice for services has not yet been analyzed. Referring to the findings of Wakefield and Inman (2003), i.e. lower price sensitivity for hedonic consumption, an impact of consumption goals on tariff choice seems very likely.

2.3 Flat-Rate Bias Consequences and Competitive Position[2]

2.3.1 Flat-Rate Bias Consequences

Once flat-rate bias led to flat-rate choice, the question is: what are the consequences—is this a sustainable situation? The only research study explicitly analyzing consequences of flat-rate bias is the work of Lambrecht and Skiera (2006). Based on three months transactional data of 10,882 DSL customers they identify customers with flat-rate bias using two criteria: The less strict criterion "overall" defines flat-rate bias if a customer would have saved money in sum over all the three months, the stricter criterion "always" requires savings from switching to pay-per-use in every single month. Using criterion "overall", no impact of flat-rate bias on switching and churn can be observed. Only under the stricter criterion "always" the analysis shows an increased tariff switching on a 10% significance level but still no impact on churn. Thus their conclusion is that customers are "paying too much and being happy about it" (Lambrecht & Skiera, 2006, p. 212).

Using these results they estimate the impact of flat-rate bias on the company's profits. They compare the actual profits of flat-rate bias customers with the profits they would have produced using the least costly tariff. The results indicate that customers with flat-rate bias have a substantially higher Customer Lifetime Value than customers in the least costly tariff. This would mean that there would be no need for service providers to act.

However, their analysis is based on a very short observation window of three months. When compared to a typical lifetime of Internet Service Provider (ISP) customers of several years, this time span might be too short to measure flat-rate bias sufficiently accurate. Also it is likely that they cannot capture customers' reactions completely, since typically service providers have a notice period of one or two months for contract cancellations. Additionally, their research does not follow a

[2] This chapter is based on joint research with Felix Frank.

longitudinal cohort-based approach which is especially important for studying customer defection rates (Reinartz & Kumar, 2000).

Besides flat-rate bias, there also exists pay-per-use bias—when customers choose a pay-per-use tariff although a flat-rate would be less expensive for them. Lambrecht and Skiera (2006) calculated the impact of this type of bias on customer retention, switching and profits. In contrast to flat-rate bias, pay-per-use bias significantly increases churn und subsequently leads in the long-term to lower profits. Combining the results of flat-rate and pay-per-use bias still shows an overall positive effect on customer profitability in the long-term.

Other studies do not differentiate between pay-per-use and flat-rate bias. They look at the consequences of wrong tariff choices in general. Their results show that customers who have chosen the economically wrong tariff have lower retention rates than customers who have chosen the right tariff (Joo et al., 2002; Wong, 2010b). Joo, Jun and Kim (2002) analyze the bills of 10,000 randomly selected mobile telecommunications customers. 40% have subscribed to the wrong calling plan. Estimating profit implications they find out that it is possible to increase overall profits when migrating selected customers with tariff biases to the respective least costly tariffs as the lower churn rates compensate the loss of higher short-term profits in the long-term. Wong (2010) analyzes payment records of 1,403 Canadian mobile telecommunications users. 46 % of them overpay with their selected tariffs. His results also indicate that churn rates are significantly higher for customers with the wrong calling plan than for customers with the right. This seems plausible as customers who become aware of the wrong tariff choice might not only question their tariff but also their provider to whom they potentially attribute this failure (Peterson et al., 1982; Riess et al., 1981).

2.3.2 Competitive Position

A main driver of customer loyalty is the attractiveness of competitive offers (Morgan & Hunt, 1994). Customers churn if they find more attractive, cheaper tariffs in the market. The potential savings by competitive offers are determined by the competitive position of the service provider.

Michael Porter (1980) defined three generic business level strategies that determine the competitive position of a service provider: differentiation, cost leadership, and focus. The latter one can be seen as a special case of the first two just with a narrow market scope (D'Aveni, 1994). This lead to controversial discussions in academia regarding the value add of distinguishing the focus strategy (Murray, 1988; Porter, 1985). Therefore this dissertation focuses only on the first two oppositional strategies (cost leadership and differentiation) which are performed by low-cost and premium providers respectively.

A differentiation strategy means offering products or services differentiated by unique characteristics such as the service quality or the service level at a relatively high price (Dess & Davis, 1984). To achieve this differentiation, premium telecommunications providers, for instance, operate own technical infrastructure achieving a high service level, fast and reliable connection quality, and offer superior customer service such as 24h hotlines, a large shop network with wide geographical reach. Another good example of a premium service provider is the Deutsche Lufthansa AG in the aviation sector. They differentiate themselves from competition by a highly professional in flight service, free beverages and food, Miles and More as customer retention program, and many other criteria (Viellechner, 2010). For such quality leaders it is important to maintain their unique competitive advantages over time. They typically attract customers with low price sensitivity that rather look for quality (C. W. L. Hill, 1988; Murray, 1988) and accept high prices (Porter, 1980). But this also leaves more space for potential savings from competitors.

A cost leadership strategy instead aims at offering services at the lowest price in the market or at least the lowest price to value ratio (Porter, 1980). In order to achieve low prices, low-cost providers typically offer no-frills services. This means acceptable quality without extra services at the lowest price or at least the lowest price to value ratio in the target market. In operations, low-cost providers need to be highly efficient and rather focus on cost optimization than on service quality. In the telecommunications sector, low-cost providers do not own a physical retail network and offer only online or telephone service. In the aviation sector, a good example would be Ryanair—the probably most prominent low-cost carrier in the market. They operate with no frills service level where customers have to pay extra for luggage or food (Viellechner, 2010). Customers of low-cost service providers are typically characterized by high price sensitivity (C. W. L. Hill, 1988; Murray, 1988) being attracted by the low prices. This means that savings from competitive offers are limited by definition in this market segment.

The concept of generic strategies has been criticized by various researchers for being oversimplified and not practically applicable. Yet, it is a good concept to describe basic strategic directions and explains the success of some companies and the miss-success of others in many cases (C. W. L. Hill, 1988; Murray, 1988). It can be used to show how firms can create a competitive advantage in order to outperform the industry (Dess & Davis, 1984). It can also help to better understand industry dynamics in terms of hypercompetition (D'Aveni, 1994).

A differentiation of the consequences of flat-rate bias based on the competitive position of the service provider has not been made so far. Although it could resolve the converse findings of Lambrecht and Skiera (2006) with general research on tariff choice (Joo et al., 2002; Wong, 2010b), as it determines the attractiveness of competitive offers which is a main driver for loyalty (Morgan & Hunt, 1994).

3 Impact of Consumption Goals on Flat-Rate Bias

3.1 Hypotheses Development

3.1.1 Impact on Convenience Effect

The convenience effect can be explained by transaction cost theory (Nunes, 2000), driven by search and handling costs. When choosing a tariff, customers tend to minimize their search cost (Lambrecht & Skiera, 2006). If the tariff structure is complex, customers need to exert effort to estimate their expected usage and calculate the respective costs (Winer, 2005).

The more hedonic the consumption goal, the more emotional and less rational the decision mode that customers adopt; They are less willing to spend time investigating the tariff logic and calculating the expected cost of pay-per-use pricing (Khan et al., 2004). With utilitarian consumption goals, consumers rely on a more rational and less emotional decision mode (Andersson & Engelberg, 2006). Therefore, customers are more willing to think through the pay-per-use pricing schemes:

H_1: The convenience effect is stronger in a hedonic than in a utilitarian setting.

3.1.2 Impact on Taxi-Meter Effect

Three differences mark hedonic versus utilitarian consumption that relate to the taxi-meter effect. First, as shown before, hedonic benefits like pleasure, fun, and enjoyment arise already during the process of consumption (Batra & Ahtola, 1991). Such services could also be called "experience-centric services" and are characterized by an intense emotional customer participation level and a constant flow of benefits (Zomerdijk & Voss, 2009). The instrumental value of utilitarian consumption instead occurs only once, after consumption (Khan et al., 2004).

Second, in addition to the financial pain of paying, hedonic services evoke a feeling of guilt and a need to justify spending money on fun and enjoyment (Okada, 2005), for reasons such as anticipated regret, cognitive dissonance, or rational self-perception. Hedonic services seem like luxuries, and consuming them often is associated with negative self-attribution (e.g., “I indulge”). It is harder to justify spending money on hedonic than on utilitarian services, which are necessities and usually have a clear purpose (Khan et al., 2004). These negative feelings lower the enjoyment from consumption to some degree though the overall benefit still remains positively hedonic by nature. However, if the payment is decoupled from consumption through a flat-rate, the enjoyment would be higher.

Third, the pain of paying lowers enjoyment, which is the main benefit sought from hedonic consumption (O'Curry & Strahilevitz, 2001). In a utilitarian context, the main benefit is independent of hedonic enjoyment (Prelec & Loewenstein, 1998), so the pain of paying should be lower in the utilitarian compared with the hedonic context.

H_2: The taxi-meter effect is stronger in a hedonic than in a utilitarian setting.

3.1.3 Impact on Insurance Effect

The insurance effect is driven by risk aversion, loss aversion, and an option value. Risk-averse behavior emerges when people prefer a flat-rate because they fear the uncertainty that they might pay more (Miravete, 2000; Nunes, 2000; Train, 1991) Under loss aversion, those situations of paying more would be perceived so bad that the positive feelings from situations of paying less cannot compensate for. For hedonic goods, the risk of losses should be perceived as worse than that for utilitarian goods, because feelings of guilt and justification extend beyond a financial perspective (Okada, 2005).

The option value of a flat-rate describes the possibility that the customer will consume more than originally planned, at the same price (Kridel et al., 1993). If the desired level of consumption is met or exceeded, consumers value hedonic attributes more than utilitarian attributes (Chitturi et al., 2007). The excess consumption (=option value) then seems like a prize won in the lottery. O'Curry and Strahilevitz (2001) show that hedonic options are more popular prizes than utilitarian ones. Thus, the option value of hedonic consumption is expected to be higher as well. Therefore:

H_3: The insurance effect is stronger in a hedonic than in a utilitarian setting.

3.1.4 Impact on Overestimation Effect

The overestimation effect is a result of an inaccurate demand forecast. Due to Paraducci's range-frequency model, people perceive a higher likelihood of consuming more than of consuming less (Nunes, 2000).

Affect-rich, hedonic services create stronger associative imagery than affect-poor, utilitarian services (Khan et al., 2004). This strong associative imagery induces an emotional decision mode, whereas a lack of imagery fosters a rational evaluation (Kahneman & Frederick, 2002). The more rational the evaluation, the more people calculate their usage; the more emotional the evaluation, the higher the likelihood that they use Paraducci's range-frequency model.

If they have used the service before, consumers can predict the frequency of future usage, based on their prior behavior. An easy retrieval of historic usage information implies a higher usage frequency (Tversky & Kahneman, 1973). More detailed or vivid historic usage information is easier to retrieve. Because hedonic consumption is more emotionally laden than utilitarian consumption, it is easier to retrieve (Carroll, 1978). Thus:

H_4: The overestimation effect is stronger in a hedonic than in a utilitarian setting.

3.1.5 Impact on Tariff Choice

Finally, according to Lambrecht and Skiera (2006), the flat-rate bias results from the combination of the four flat-rate bias effects—from which the most significant explanation comes from the taxi-meter, insurance, and overestimation effects. With increasing effect sizes, the flat-rate bias grows. Because all predictions about the impact of the consumption goal on the individual effects imply stronger effect sizes in a hedonic context, the flat-rate bias, as an outcome of these effects, should also be stronger in a hedonic than in a utilitarian setting:

H_5: The flat-rate bias is stronger in a hedonic than in a utilitarian setting.

3.1.6 Relationship between Consumption Goals and Tariff Choice

Knowing that consumption goals influence flat-rate bias effects and tariff choice is not enough, it is also important to understand how: The mechanism how independent variables function together influencing the dependent variable is an important finding (Hayes & Preacher, 2011). As consumption goals impact both, flat-rate bias effects and flat-rate choice, the relationship between the consumption goals and flat-rate bias effects shall be investigated further. Either consumption goals moderate the relationship between flat-rate bias effects and tariff choice, or flat-rate bias effects are mediators for the consumption goals (Baron & Kenny, 1986).

As hypotheses H_1 to H_4 predict a direct increase of flat-rate bias effect size based on hedonic consumption goals, and the four effects themselves again have proven to increase flat-rate bias, it is expected that the four effects act as mediators between consumption goals and flat-rate bias. Specifically, the consumption goals should have an indirect impact on flat-rate choice that is fully mediated by the flat-rate bias effects. Hedonic consumption increases the flat-rate bias effects and hence indirectly flat-rate bias much stronger than utilitarian consumption. Thus:

H_6: The impact of the consumption goals on flat-rate choice is fully mediated by the flat-rate bias effects.

3.1.7 Impact on Willingness to Pay

A potential recommendation based on the hypotheses would be to "hedonize" service offerings in order to artificially increase flat-rate bias and subsequently profits. To make sure, the "hedonization" of services has no negative side effects on profits, the impact on customers' willingness to pay should be taken into account as well. Shiv, Carmon, and Ariely (2005) for example argue that marketing activities such as price discounts may have negative effects on customer expectations in terms of product benefits and even actually perceived product efficacy. A lower price might signal lower quality to consumers and therefore they do not trust in the efficacy anymore. Applied to this research this could mean that stressing hedonic benefits with marketing actions might have negative effects on the perceived efficacy of the service for consumers which might lower the willingness to pay.

In contrast, from the area of price sensitivity research, Wakefield and Inman (Wakefield & Inman, 2003) suggest that consumers are more willing to pay for hedonic than for utilitarian products and services. In a similar vein, Gill (2008) argues that convergent products gain more value from hedonic than from utilitarian add-ons. He compares the willingness to pay for several convergent base products and adds new functionalities to them. Independent of the nature of the base products, hedonic add-ons consistently increase the willingness to pay more than utilitarian add-ons. Therefore, besides an increase of flat-rate bias, hedonic context is expected to also result in higher willingness to pay:

H_7: The willingness to pay is higher for hedonic services than for utilitarian.

3.1.8 Overview of Hypotheses H_1 to H_7

Table 3 gives an overview on all hypotheses developed in the previous chapters. Hypotheses H_1 to H_4 thereby predict higher flat-rate bias effects in hedonic contexts which fully mediate the impact of consumption goals (H_6) on tariff choice such that flat-rate bias is stronger in a hedonic compared to a utilitarian consumption situation (H_5). Hypothesis H_7 furthermore predicts higher willingness to pay for hedonic services.

Hypothesis	*Relevant Element*	*Prediction*
H_1	Convenience effect	Hed > Ut
H_2	Taxi-meter effect	Hed > Ut
H_3	Insurance effect	Hed > Ut
H_4	Overestimation effect	Hed > Ut
H_5	Flat-rate bias	Hed > Ut
H_6	Relationship	Full mediation
H_7	Willingness to Pay	Hed > Ut

Table 3—Overview of Hypotheses H_1 to H_7

Figure 5 represents these hypotheses in a conceptual research model.

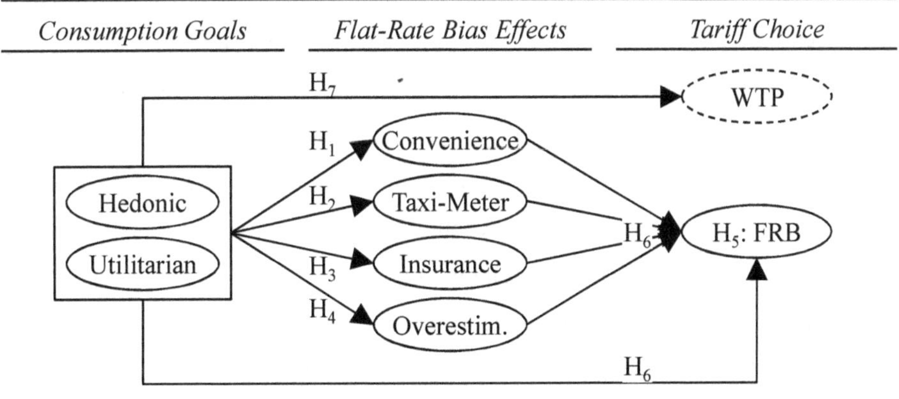

Figure 5—Conceptual Research Model for Hypotheses H_1 to H_7

3.2 Empirical Study

3.2.1 Research Approach and Methodology

To determine the individual impact of hedonic and utilitarian consumption goals, flat-rate bias effects and flat-rate choice must be compared in three conditions (Carson et al., 1994): pure hedonic, hybrid hedonic and utilitarian, and pure utilitarian tariff choices. To generate these conditions in experimental surveys, the following approaches were applied in five studies to combine their respective strengths and eliminate their weaknesses.

Study 1. The first study compares different services. This results in realistic conditions as real services can be used, and at the same time achieves a wide spread of consumption goals. However, it is critical to ensure that the services only differ in the perceived consumption goal, not in other criteria, such as price level or usage frequency.

Study 2 & 3. These two studies use artificial variance created by hypothetical scenarios in which respondents make a decision for another person. In these consumption situations the hedonic and utilitarian dimensions of the third person can be designed freely to achieve a maximum spread. At the same time it can be ensured via the scenario description that all other elements are equal. However, because respondents make the tariff choice for a third person, the results might have limited validity (Epley, Savitsky, & Gilovich, 2002).

Study 4 & 5. Therefore, the natural consumption goal variance of different respondents toward the same service gets leveraged. This ensures the comparability of service characteristics but limits the spectrum of hedonic–utilitarian ratings (Carson et al., 1994). While studies 1 to 3 will be mainly analyzed with group comparisons of tariff choice and flat-rate bias effects, studies 4 and 5 allow for additionally testing of the mediation hypothesis using multiple regressions as hed/ut ratings are ordinal scaled and not based on groups.

In order to test H_7 (impact of consumption goals on the willingness to pay), a further study (*Study 6*) uses one service primed with different advertisements to generate three experimental conditions: pure hedonic, pure utilitarian, and hybrid. Potential customers of the service then need to provide information on their willingness to pay for the three services and group differences can be analyzed.

Studies 1, 2, and 4 were conducted with a paper based questionnaire during a marketing lecture at a large university in South Germany in summer 2010. As motivation to participate in the survey, students received candy after completing the three studies which were stacked in one questionnaire with randomized order. Study 3 was conducted online by the marketing research agency Research Now (RN) in autumn 2010. The sample was quoted to represent the German population in terms of gender, age, education, and income. For Study 5, Research Now was mandated again in summer 2011 to recruit another representative sample excluding participants of the first experiment. Also this sample had to fulfill the same quotas and answered to the questionnaire via the internet. Subjects for Study 6 were recruited online via e-mails and postings in social networks as a convenience sample consisting mainly of friends and family (FnF). Table 4 provides an overview of the approaches used in the various studies. The selection of services used for the respective approaches is described in Chapter 3.2.3.

	Research Approach				*Hypothesis Tests*		
Study	*Hed/Ut Variance*	*Service*	*Decision Subject*	*Sample*	$H_{1\text{-}5}$	H_6	H_7
1	Two services	Amusement park vs. public transportation	Respondent	Students	X		
2	Hypothetical scenarios	Dance lessons	Third person	Students	X	X	
3		Thermal bath visit	Third person	RN1	X	X	
4	Natural variance	Thermal bath visit	Respondent	Students	X	X	
5		Energy museum visit	Respondent	RN2	X	X	
6	Priming	Thermal bath visit	Respondent	FnF			X

Notes: N(Students) = 268, N(RN1) = 298, N(RN2) = 376, N(FnF) = 194

Table 4—Overview of Research Approaches

3.2.2 Research Design

In all tariff choice experiments (Studies 1 to 5), respondents first read a description of the choice situation to make the task more realistic (Carson et al., 1994), such as, "suppose you are about to enter an amusement park and have the choice of two price rates." Respondents then get asked to decide between flat-rate and pay-per-use pricing. A four-point scale (1 = "definitely pay-per-use," 2 = "probably pay-per-use," 3 = "probably flat-rate," and 4 = "definitely flat-rate") was used instead of a binary decision to better measure weak signals and preferences between the two options. The payment modalities were the same for both rates, to eliminate any impact of personal preferences regarding payment methods. As a decision support and guidance, respondents were told to presume a given usage pattern, outlined by a range from minimum to maximum expected usage (e.g., minimum three rides, maximum nine rides). Also the expected usage as an arithmetic mean (e.g., on average, six rides) was provided. The flat-rate price always equaled the average usage multiplied by the pay-per-use price, following the definition of flat-rate bias by Train (1991). If there were no flat-rate bias, half the respondents should choose pay-per-use pricing and the other half the flat-rate. This procedure mirrors other flat-rate bias research (e.g., Lambrecht & Skiera, 2006). The prices and usage patterns came from desk research and pretests, which indicated typical values, to make the decisions as realistic as possible.

After revealing the tariff choice, flat-rate bias effects were measured on a five-point scale (1 = "fully disagree," 5 = "fully agree"). The scales for the convenience, taxi-meter, and insurance effects were based on the reflective measurement scales from Lambrecht and Skiera (2006), and adjusted to the specifics of each service for every experiment and translated into German. For the overestimation effect, a new four-item scale was developed that appears, together with the other scales, in Table 5.

Effect/Scale, Item	
Convenience	
• It is too much effort for me to estimate whether paying by hour or taking the day-pass is cheaper for me.	c1
• The money I can save with the right tariff is not worth the time and effort for an extensive analysis of tariffs.	c2
• The time it takes to calculate which tariff is better is not worth it.*	c3
Taxi-Meter	
• The day-pass for the energy museum is great because I don't need to think about the cost every hour.	t1
• I enjoy visiting the energy museum less if costs rise every hour.*	t2
• Only with a day-pass do I have real fun in the energy museum.*	t3
• If I have a day-pass I feel much more free and unstressed visiting the energy museum than having a variable rate.	t4
• I don't like it if costs increase every hour.*	t5
Insurance	
• For the security that the energy museum visit never exceeds a preset price, I'd even pay a bit more.	i1
• Even if the day-pass would be a bit more expensive for me I'd be happy because my total cost will never exceed a fixed amount.	i2
• The transparency of knowing in advance how much the energy museum visit will cost me is important to me.*	i3
• It is important that the visit never costs more than a fixed amount.*	i4
• I don't like it if costs are higher than originally planned.*	i5
Overestimation	
• I can well imagine spending more time in the museum than on average.	o1
• The probability to spend more time in the museum is higher than the probability to spend less time in the museum.	o2
• The case that I stay longer in the museum happens more often than the case that I stay shorter.*	o3
• The risk of visiting the museum for longer than average is higher than the risk of visiting the museum for shorter than average.*	o4
Hedonic	
• Visiting the energy museum is fun.	h1
• Visiting the energy museum is exciting.	h2
• Visiting the energy museum is delightful.	h3
• Visiting the energy museum is thrilling.	h4
• Visiting the energy museum is enjoyable.	h5
Utilitarian	
• Visiting the energy museum is effective.	u1
• Visiting the energy museum is helpful.	u2
• Visiting the energy museum is functional.	u3
• Visiting the energy museum is necessary.	u4
• Visiting the energy museum is practical.	u5

* Item not included in reduced scale of Studies 1, 2, and 4 to shorten survey.

Table 5—Measurement Scales for Flat-Rate Bias Effects and Consumption Goals

As manipulation check, and to analyze the natural variance of consumption goals, every respondent's consumption goal was measured at the end of the survey (Perdue & Sommers, 1986). For this purpose, the well-established hed/ut scale (see Table 5) by Voss, Spangenberg, and Grohmann (2003) gets used, translated into German. Both hedonic and utilitarian consumption goals for the service were measured on a five-point scale (1 = "fully disagree," 5 = "fully agree") (Khan et al., 2004).

To measure the willingness to pay in study 6, open ended questions were used asking respondents for the amount of Euro they would be willing to spend for a day pass. Miller et al. (2011) compare several methods to capture customers' willingness to pay with real purchase data—from choice-based conjoint analysis, to incentive-compatible mechanism, to incentive-aligned choice-based conjoint analysis, to open-ended questions. Their results indicate that though open-ended questions generate some hypothetical bias, they are still able to derive the right pricing decisions. Therefore, this easy-to-implement format was used as the method of choice.

As confound check (Perdue & Sommers, 1986), the attitude towards the advertisements was measured in Study 6 based on the Aad-scale used by Biehal, Stephens, and Curio (1992). The subjects' Aad score was calculated as the average of five 5-point scales: good/bad, like/dislike, interesting/boring, creative/uncreative, and informative/uninformative.

All scales were tested using exploratory (SPSS version 18) and confirmatory (AMOS version 18 with maximum likelihood algorithm) factor analyses. The quality criterions the scales had to pass in these analyses were the following: The Kaiser criterion—indicating the number of extracted factors—must be one for all scales to make sure that each scale measures only one factor. And this one factor needs to explain at least 50% of all scale's items variances (Bagozzi & Yi, 1988). The KMO Bartlett test of at least .6 (Cureton & D'Agostino, 1983) proves a strong relationship of the items with the scale (factor). Minimum factor loadings of .5 (Bagozzi & Yi, 1988) ensure high convergent validity. A Cronbachs Alpha larger than .7 indicates internal consistency of the scale's items (Nunnally, 1978) and thus ensures the reliability of the scale. Thereby, all corrected item to total correlations are supposed to be higher or equal than .5 (Bearden, Netemeyer, & Mobley, 1993).

Furthermore, the confirmatory factor analysis requires indicator reliabilities bigger than .4 (Bagozzi & Baumgartner, 1994) for all items of the scale. And factor reliability must be larger or equal .6 with an average variance extracted of minimum .5 (Bagozzi & Yi, 1988). Finally, the Fornell/Larcker criterion (Fornell & Larcker, 1981) had to be met for all tests to ensure discriminant validity.

3.2.3 Pretest: Identifying Services for Tariff Choice Experiments

A pretest should reveal suitable services for the experiments. Based on the official German services catalogue as a starting point, a long list of 40 consumer services got extracted with a focus on services that potentially could be offered under flat-rate and pay-per-use pricing (see Table 6).

To select services for direct comparison (Study 1), pairs of services that differ in their consumption goals but are equal in all other regards (ceteris paribus) were to be found. Otherwise, ulterior dominant alternatives might distort the tariff choice (Carson et al., 1994; Krieger & Green, 1991). The following six criteria were developed to ensure ceteris paribus: (1) Contractual setting: Both services need to be available on the identical contractual setting, e.g., subscription model (per month/year) versus one-time purchase. (2) Integrated factor: Service consumption is characterized by the close integration of the customer or his belongings in the production/consumption process (Zeithaml et al., 2010). For comparability, equal level of integration (i.e. direct = the customer versus indirect = his belongings) is necessary. (3) Time frame: Also the time frame for service consumption should be comparable (i.e. monthly flat versus one-year contract). (4) Price level: Furthermore, a similar price level (i.e. order of magnitude) is prerequisite for direct service comparison. (5) Frequency: The frequency and usage cycles should be in a comparable range. It is not possible to compare a season ticket for soccer with one match every week with a season ticket for the opera with one play per night. (6) Variability: Finally the variability of deviations from the expected usage should be similar. Comparing car repairs with more or less binary occurrence probability with annual drinking water demand that has very low variability would bias the decision.

Service	*Contractual Setting*	*Int. Fact*	*Time frame*	*€ Price Level*	*Fre-quency*	*Varia-bility*
Amusement park*	Once/Subs.	Direct	d/y	30/360	8[a]/96[a]	33%
Cable TV	Subscript.	Ind.	m	20	16[b]	33%
Car fuel	Subscript.	Ind.	y	600-3K	12-36[c]	10%
Car service	Once/Subs.	Ind.	y	500	1[c]	100%
Car wash*	Once/Subs.	Ind.	y	120	12[c]	33%
Cinema*	Subscript.	Direct	y	192	24[d]	33%
Coupon clubs	Subscript.	Direct	y	60	12[c]	33%
Cultural event*	Subscript.	Direct	y	360	12[d]	33%
Dancing club*	Subscript.	Direct	y	360	36[d]	33%
Doctor visit	Once/Subs.	Direct	y	250-3K	4[d]	100%
Energy supply	Subscript.	Ind.	y	>360	360[e]	10%
Equipment rental	Once	Ind.	d	50-1K	1-12[c]	100%
Fitness center	Subscript.	Direct	m/y	100/1K	4/48[d]	33%
Food buffet	Once	Direct	d	30	-	33%
Fun bath*	Once/Subs.	Direct	d/y	30/720	4[b]/96[b]	33%
Gardener service	Once/Subs.	Ind.	d/y	50-1K	6[c]	10%
Geothermal bath*	Once/Subs.	Direct	d/y	30/720	4[b]/96[b]	33%
Insurances	Once/Subs.	D/I	d/y	10-3K	4[f]	100%
Laundry service*	Subscript.	Ind.	y	500	100[c]	33%
Library	Subscript.	Direct	y	60	30[g]	33%
Lymph drainage	Once/Subs.	Direct	m	240	8[c]	33%
Magazines	Subscript.	Direct	y	60	12[h]	33%
Maid-service	Subscript.	Ind.	y	>1K	48[d]	33%
Mobile internet*	Once/Subs.	Ind.	m/y	25/300	30/360[b]	33%
Museum*	Once/Subs.	Direct	d/y	20/240	4[b]/12[d]	33%
Music download	Subscript.	Ind.	m/y	10/120	8[h]/96[h]	33%
Online brokerage	Subscript.	Ind.	m/y	10/120	4[i]/48[i]	33%
Public transport*	Once/Subs.	Direct	d/m	6/120	4[j]/80[j]	33%
Research database	Subscript.	Ind.	y	50-1K	8[h]/96[h]	33%
Residential parking	Subscript.	Ind.	m/y	10/120	20/240[e]	33%
Sauna club	Once/Subs.	Direct	d/y	30/720	4[b]/96[b]	33%
Ski-lift*	Once/Subs.	Direct	d/y	30/360	10[j]/100[j]	33%
Sport massage	Subscript.	Direct	m	240	8[c]	33%
Sports club*	Subscript.	Direct	m/y	100/1K	8[d]/96[d]	33%
Sports season ticket	Subscript.	Direct	y	600	2[d]/24[d]	33%
Taxi rides	Once	Direct	d	20-200	5-50[k]	33%
Travel office	Once	Direct	y	50-500	2[i]	33%
Video downloads	Subscript.	Ind.	m/y	20/240	8[h]/96[h]	33%
Water supply	Subscript.	Ind.	y	360	360[e]	10%
Wellness massage	Subscript.	Direct	m	240	8[b]	33%

* Selected for short list, [a] rides, [b] hours, [c] applications, [d] visits, [e] days, [f] instances, [g] lendings, [h] pieces, [i] transactions, [j] rides, [k] kilometers.

Notes: d = day, m = month, y = year, ind. = indirect.

Table 6—Short- and Long-List of Services for Tariff Choice Experiments

Brainstorming with service experts of an international consulting firm, the 40 services were classified along the six criteria assuming typical users for the service.

Those criteria were important to find a "ceteris paribus" service pair for study 1. Based on the pervasiveness and familiarity of the service, and the possibility for flat-rate and pay-per-use pricing, the long-list was cut to 13 services (see Table 6, services market with *).

In an online survey, 62 respondents rated the hedonic and utilitarian consumption goals of the 13 short-listed services (see Figure 6). They identified dancing lessons, geothermal baths and museum visits as the most balanced services regarding hedonic and utilitarian consumption goals. This classified those three services to be used for Studies 2, 3, 4 and 5. Furthermore, two services with strongly oppositional consumption goals were identified: Amusement parks are purely hedonic, public transportation is solely utilitarian. In most other regards, both services are quite similar: The time frame of one day and the contractual setting of not being bound by a contract are identical. Both services require the consumer to involve personally and physically during consumption by sitting in a train / coach. And the obtained typical usage patterns and price levels from the pre-test survey are in a similar order of magnitude. Hence, those two services were used for study 1. Study 6 leveraged the thermal bath visit.

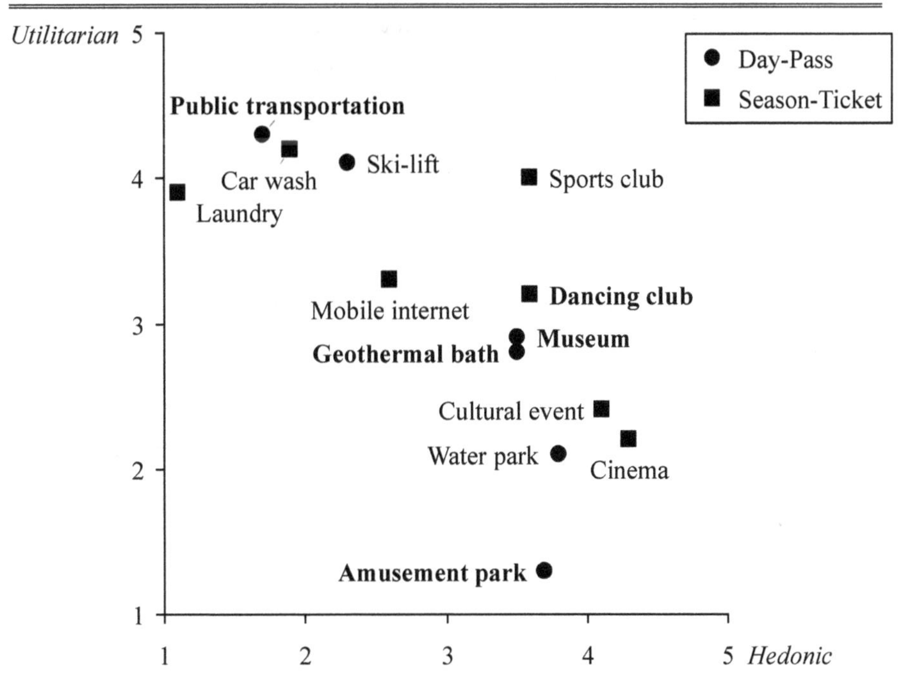

Figure 6—Hed/Ut Ratings of Short-Listed Services

3.2.4 Study 1: Hypothetical Public Transportation and Amusement Park Rides

3.2.4.1 Description of Experimental Setup and Sample

Paper based questionnaires were handed out to all students of an undergraduate marketing course at a large university in south Germany in summer 2010 (see Appendix A). As a reward for their participation, students received candies. All in all 268 completed questionnaires were obtained. Table 7 shows the age and gender distribution of the students:

Criterion	*Value*	*%*
Gender	Male	64%
	Female	36%
Age	< 20 years	9%
	20 years	38%
	21 years	30%
	22 years	8%
	> 22 years	15%

Table 7—Socio-Demographic Characteristics of Respondents for Study 1, 2, and 4

The two settings (buying a ticket for an amusement park visit versus running some errands across the city using public transportation) appeared in random order (together with further experiments as used in Studies 2 and 4). In both experiments, students rated their preference for a day pass versus paying per ride. A past usage pattern was provided with minimum, average, and maximum rides per day (public transportation 2–4–6; amusement park 4–8–12). The price for the day pass reflected the average usage, yielding realistic prices for this university town (e.g., public transportation €2 per ride × 4 rides = €8 per day; amusement park €3 per ride × 8 rides = €24 per day).

In addition, the students completed the flat-rate bias effects and consumption goal scales. In order to keep the overall time for completing the questionnaire as short as possible despite the within subject design comparing two services, the flat-rate bias effects scales were reduced to two items each.

3.2.4.2 Measurement Scale Validation and Manipulation Checks

First, all measurement scales need to be validated with exploratory and confirmatory factor analysis. The results (see Table 8) indicate for both services that the measurement constructs work well to capture the latent constructs. Only in the public transportation scenario, the taxi-meter effect scale does not meet .5 average variance extracted in the CFA. This might be due to the fact that using public transportation is not related to fun and enjoyment at all.

	Public Transportation				*Amusement Parks*			
Effect/Scale	*α*	*EV*	*FR*	*AVE*	*α*	*EV*	*FR*	*AVE*
Item	CITC	FL	SRW	IR	CITC	FL	SRW	IR
Convenience	*.61*	*.72*	*.61*	*.44*	*.65*	*.74*	*.72*	*.59*
c1*	.44	.85	.71	.50	.49	.86	.51	.26
c2*	.44	.85	.62	.38	.49	.86	.95	.90
Taxi-Meter	*.56*	*.43*	*.54*	*.37*	*.72*	*.55*	*.65*	*.49*
t1*	.35	.68	.57	.32	.53	.75	.65	.42
t4*	.47	.79	.65	.42	.62	.80	.74	.55
Insurance	*.65*	*.74*	*.65*	*.48*	*.67*	*.75*	*.66*	*.50*
i1*	.48	.86	.69	.48	.50	.87	.70	.49
i2*	.48	.86	.70	.49	.50	.87	.71	.50
Overestimation	*.70*	*.77*	*.70*	*.54*	*.75*	*.80*	*.75*	*.60*
o1*	.54	.88	.79	.62	.60	.90	.79	.62
o2*	.54	.88	.68	.46	.60	.90	.76	.58
Hedonic	*.85*	*.63*	*.84*	*.51*	*.93*	*.78*	*.93*	*.72*
h1	.65	.77	.75	.56	.86	.92	.91	.83
h2	.66	.80	.60	.36	.84	.90	.88	.77
h3	.67	.79	.78	.61	.80	.87	.84	.71
h4	.67	.81	.62	.38	.76	.85	.79	.62
h5	.70	.82	.80	.64	.79	.87	.83	.69
Utilitarian	*.82*	*.59*	*.82*	*.47*	*.87*	*.67*	*.87*	*.58*
u1	.68	.81	.81	.66	.67	.79	.75	.56
u2	.63	.77	.63	.40	.76	.85	.82	.67
u3	.65	.79	.73	.53	.71	.82	.75	.56
u4	.57	.73	.67	.45	.65	.78	.71	.50
u5	.58	.74	.58	.34	.72	.84	.78	.61
Fit Indices	*RMSEA*	χ^2/df	*TLI*	*CFI*	*RMSEA*	χ^2/df	*TLI*	*CFI*
	.06	1.90	.92	.89	.06	1.86	.94	.95

Notes: *α* = Cronbach's Alpha, CITC = Corrected Item-to-Total Correlation, *EV* = Explained Variance, FL = Factor Loading, *FR* = Factor Reliability, SRW = Standardized Regression Weight, *AVE* = Average Variance Extracted, IR = Indicator Reliability. KMO & Bartelett test met, Fornell/Larcker criterion met (except for taxi-meter effect: correlation with insurance effect leads to negative Fornell/Larcker ratio of -.08). * Reduced set of items to shorten survey.

Table 8—EFA & CFA for Hypothetical Public Transportation and Amusement Park Rides

The manipulation check using two dependent samples T-tests confirms the pretested classification of both services: The amusement park is perceived as significantly more hedonic (M = 3.8, SE = .06) than public transportation (M = 1.8, SE = .04, T(243) = –30.0, p < .001), whereas public transportation appears significantly more utilitarian (M = 4.0, SE = .05) than amusement parks (M = 1.8, SE = .05, T(243) = 29.1, p < .001). Figure 7 shows the hedonic and utilitarian ratings of the two services:

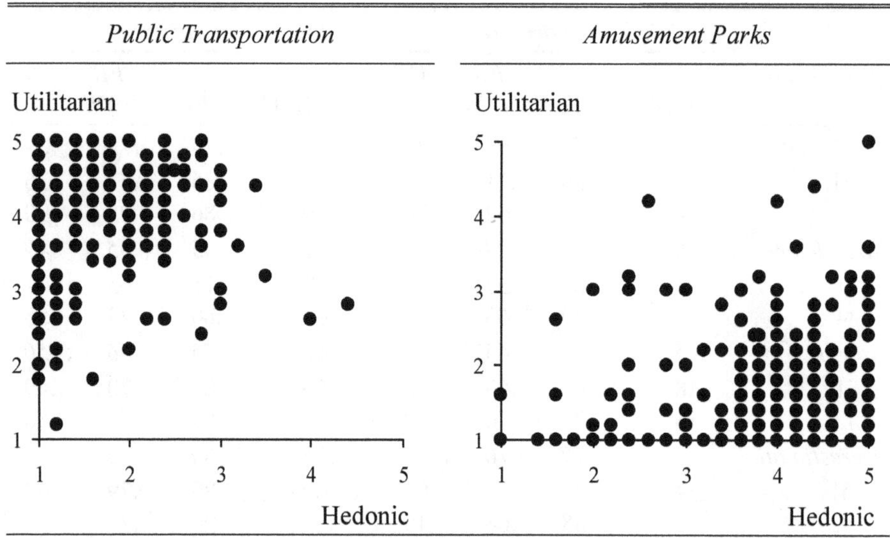

Figure 7—Hed/Ut Ratings of Hypothetical Public Transportation and Amusement Park Rides

Two linear regression models (see Table 9) show that the flat-rate bias effects explain a substantial portion of tariff choice (amusement park R^2 = .30; public transportation R^2 = .32). In the amusement park scenario, all four flat-rate bias effects are significant, whereas for public transportation only three are—overestimation has no significant impact on tariff choice. Convenience shows opposite effects in the two scenarios. For the amusement park, convenience leads to a pay-per-use preference (ß = –.11, p < .05), whereas for public transportation to flat-rate bias (ß = .12, p < .05).

	Public Transportation			Amusement Park		
	B	*SE B*	*β*	*B*	*SE B*	*β*
Constant	.78	.20		.51	.24	
Convenience	.11	.05	.12*	-.10	.05	-.11*
Taxi-meter	.34	.05	.40***	.34	.06	.34***
Insurance	.14	.05	.18**	.15	.05	.17**
Overestimation	.02	.05	.02	.23	.05	.24***
	$R^2 = .30$, $F = 27.9$***			$R^2 = .32$, $F = 30.9$***		

*$p < .05$, **$p < .01$, ***$p < .001$.
Notes: Dependent variable = tariff choice.

Table 9—Linear Regression for Hypothetical Public Transportation and Amusement Park Rides

When reducing the tariff choice scale to a binary decision (tariff choice 1 and 2 = pay-per-use, 3 and 4 = flat-rate), similar results steam from a logistic regression (see Table 10). Only the impact of the convenience effect on tariff choice becomes insignificant in this analysis.

	Public Transportation			Amusement Park		
	B	*SE B*	*Exp(B)*	*B*	*SE B*	*Exp(B)*
Constant	-5.00	.83		-5.93	1.06	
Convenience	.18	.18	1.20	-.50	.20	.60*
Taxi-meter	.96	.19	2.60***	1.04	.22	2.83***
Insurance	.45	.18	1.57*	.62	.20	1.85**
Overestimation	.18	.18	1.19	.62	.20	1.86**
	Cox & Snell $R^2 = .23$			Cox & Snell $R^2 = .27$		
	Nagelkerke $R^2 = .32$			Nagelkerke $R^2 = .38$		

*$p < .05$, **$p < .01$, ***$p < .001$.
Notes: Dependent variable = tariff choice.

Table 10—Logistic Regression for Hypothetical Public Transportation and Amusement Park Rides

3.2.4.3 Empirical Findings

Table 11 provides the results of a dependent samples T-test that compares the effects in both scenarios. The convenience effect is higher in the hedonic amusement park than in the utilitarian public transportation setting ($M_{hed} = 2.1$, $M_{ut} = 2.0$, $T(250) = -2.6$, $p < .05$) confirming H_1. Also the taxi-meter effect is higher in the amusement park than in the public transportation situation ($M_{hed} = 3.6$, $M_{ut} = 3.2$, $T(243) = -7.6$, $p < .001$). People seem to fear the loss of enjoyment much more in a hedonic than in a utilitarian context, in support of H_2. The insurance effect ($M_{hed} = 2.8$, $M_{ut} = 2.5$, $T(249) = -5.0$, $p < .001$) and the overestimation effect ($M_{hed} = 3.6$, $M_{ut} = 3.2$, $T(247)$

= –5.2, $p < .001$) are also higher in the hedonic than in the utilitarian situation, in support of H_3 and H_4. People can rather imagine doing more fun rides in the amusement park than they actually might have planned and therefore want to insure against this risk. Also they might see an option value in having the opportunity to ride more often. In the utilitarian context of public transportation, students probably only want to finish running their errands as soon as possible and do not see additional value in riding the metro more often. Regarding flat-rate choice, the students exhibit significantly higher flat-rate biases in the hedonic amusement park than in the utilitarian public transportation scenario ($M_{hed} = 2.9$, $M_{ut} = 2.6$, $T(243) = -3.7$, $p < .001$). This finding confirms H_5.

	Public Transportation		*Amusement Park*			
	M	*SE*	*M*	*SE*	*df*	*T*
Convenience	1.97	.06	2.12	.06	250	-2.58*
Taxi-meter	3.22	.04	3.60	.05	250	-7.35***
Insurance	2.48	.06	2.79	.06	249	-4.97***
Overestimation	3.19	.06	3.58	.06	247	-5.22***
Tariff choice	2.63	.05	2.88	.06	241	-3.65***

*$p < .05$, **$p < .01$, ***$p < .001$.

Table 11—Dependent Samples T-Test for Hypothetical Public Transportation and Amusement Park Rides

3.2.4.4 Summary of Study 1

Study 1 reveals that a flat-rate bias is stronger in a pure hedonic decision context than in a pure utilitarian decision context. To test whether this outcome is due to a change in the utilitarian or the hedonic dimension, there is a need to compare three groups in a factorial design: a pure hedonic, a pure utilitarian, and a hybrid consumption situation. Comparing the hedonic with the hybrid situation isolates the utilitarian impact; comparing the utilitarian with the hybrid isolates the hedonic impact. A neither utilitarian nor hedonic consumption situation gets avoided, because this combination is implausible and would not be treated seriously by respondents (Carson et al., 1994). Furthermore, Study 1 compares two different services. To confirm that the findings extend to other contexts, the next experiments each feature only one service.

3.2.5 Study 2: Dance Lessons Scenarios

3.2.5.1 Description of Experimental Setup and Sample

Study 2 was conducted together with study 1 using three hypothetical scenarios of a third person taking dancing lessons in a between subjects design (Bargh & Chartrand, 2000). The scenario description (see Appendix A) starts with a short text explaining the consumption goals of the third person (one of the three scenarios by randomization) for signing up a dancing class. The goal of this priming was to cause respondents put themselves into the third person's shoes and subconsciously adopt his/her consumption goal (Kolb & Whishaw, 2003). For the hedonic scenario, respondents were told that dancing is Andrea's passion. She loves moving to the rhythm of the music. She already knows all the moves perfectly and does not want to learn anything new but she still enjoys dancing. She plans to sign up for a dancing class—not to enhance her skill but just for fun. In the utilitarian scenario, Daniel is not really good at dancing and he also doesn't really like it. However, for an important event he necessarily needs to improve his skills and plans to sign up for a dancing class to study the most important moves. In the hybrid scenario, Susanne loves dancing but at the same time wants to learn new things.

For all scenarios, information about typical dance lesson visits were provided ranging from a minimum of seven, to an average of ten, to a maximum of 13 sessions per quarter. The rates were €15 per session or €150 for a quarterly pass.

3.2.5.2 Measurement Scale Validation and Manipulation Checks

Table 12 shows that all scales used in this experiment fulfill the defined fit indices. Only the scale for the convenience effect has an average variance extracted of .37 below the critical value of .5 (Bagozzi & Yi, 1988). The utilitarian scale almost reaches with .47 the .50 recommended as a rule of thumb. The overall model fit of the CFA is OK.

Effect/Scale Item	*α* CITC	*EV* FL	*FR* SRW	*AVE* IR
Convenience	*.50*	*.67*	*.53*	*.37*
c1*	.34	.82	.46	.21
c2*	.34	.82	.73	.53
Taxi-Meter	*.70*	*.77*	*.72*	*.57*
t1*	.53	.88	.88	.77
t4*	.53	.88	.61	.37
Insurance	*.69*	*.76*	*.69*	*.53*
i1*	.52	.87	.78	.61
i2*	.52	.87	.67	.45
Overestimation	*.83*	*.85*	*.85*	*.74*
o1*	.71	.92	.99	.98
o2*	.71	.92	.71	.50
Hedonic	*.97*	*.89*	*.97*	*.86*
h1	.93	.96	.96	.92
h2	.92	.95	.92	.85
h3	.93	.95	.95	.90
h4	.84	.90	.85	.72
h5	.92	.95	.95	.90
Utilitarian	*.81*	*.57*	*.81*	*.46*
u1	.65	.80	.75	.56
u2	.58	.75	.67	.45
u3	.59	.75	.67	.45
u4	.58	.74	.65	.42
u5	.58	.74	.65	.42
Fit Indices	*RMSEA*	χ^2/df	*TLI*	*CFI*
	.09	2.58	.90	.92

Notes: *α* = Cronbach's Alpha, CITC = Corrected Item-to-Total Correlation, *EV* = Explained Variance, FL = Factor Loading, *FR* = Factor Reliability, SRW = Standardized Regression Weight, *AVE* = Average Variance Extracted, IR = Indicator Reliability. KMO & Bartelett test met, Fornell/Larcker criterion met.
* Reduced set of items to shorten survey.

Table 12—EFA & CFA for Dance Lessons Scenarios

Comparing the three scenarios with two independent samples T-tests shows that the manipulation performed by the scenario descriptions has been successful. As expected, the hedonic scenario is significantly less utilitarian than the hybrid one (M_{hed} = 2.98, SE_{hed} = .09, M_{hyb} = 3.28, SE_{hyb} = .11, T(146) = 2.06, $p < .05$); there is no significant difference in hedonic perceptions between them (M_{hed} = 4.58, SE_{hed} = .06, M_{hyb} = 4.53, SE_{hyb} = .06, T(146) = –.53, $p > .05$). Accordingly, the utilitarian scenario is significantly less hedonic than the hybrid scenario (M_{ut} = 1.89, SE_{ut} = .1,1 M_{hyb} = 4.53, SE_{hyb} = .06, T(91) = –21.91, $p < .001$), and there is no significant difference in utilitarian perceptions between these two scenarios (M_{ut} = 3.38, SE_{ut} = .09, M_{hyb} = 3.28, SE_{hyb} = .11, T(125) = .70, p > .05). Thus the priming was successful. Figure 8 shows the hedonic and utilitarian ratings of the three scenarios and their averages (large symbols). One can see that the distance of the utilitarian scenario to the hybrid scenario is much larger than the distance of the hedonic to the hybrid. Therefore, this setup was repeated in Study 3 using hypothetical thermal bath visits as primed service yielding in a more equal distribution.

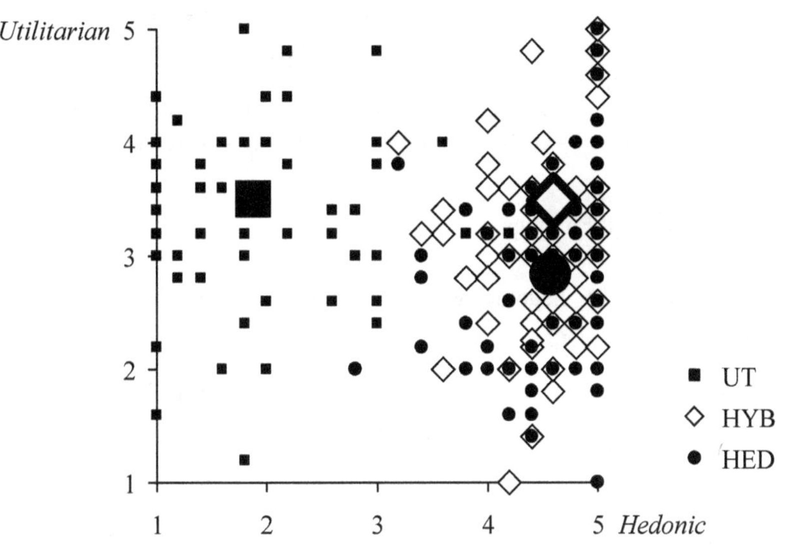

Figure 8—Hed/Ut Ratings of Dance Lessons Scenarios

A linear regression model (see Table 13) shows that the flat-rate bias effects explain a substantial portion of tariff choice (R^2 = .38). Three flat-rate bias effects are significant and support flat-rate choice. Only the convenience has no significant impact (ß = –.11, p > .08).

	B	*SE B*	*β*
Constant	.63	.25	
Convenience	-.12	.06	-.11
Taxi-meter	.22	.08	.19**
Insurance	.22	.06	.23***
Overestimation	.32	.05	.37***
	R^2 = .38, F = 33***		

*p < .05, **p < .01, ***p < .001.
Notes: Dependent variable = tariff choice.

Table 13—Linear Regression for Dance Lessons Scenarios

A logistic regression using binary tariff choice outcome (tariff choice 1 and 2 = pay-per-use, 3 and 4 = flat-rate) comes to similar results (see Table 14). Also the convenience effect is not significant with this analysis.

	B	*SE B*	*Exp(B)*
Constant	-7.68	1.35	
Convenience	-.36	.26	.70
Taxi-meter	.92	.32	2.51**
Insurance	.77	.24	2.16**
Overestimation	1.23	.22	3.43***
	Cox & Snell R^2 = .40		
	Nagelkerke R^2 = .56		

$^{**}p < .01$, $^{***}p < .001$.

Notes: Dependent variable = binary tariff choice.

Table 14—Logistic Regression for Dance Lessons Scenarios

3.2.5.3 Empirical Findings

Comparing the hedonic with the utilitarian scenario using independent samples T-tests (see Table 15) shows that the taxi-meter (M_{hed} = 3.4, M_{ut} = 2.8, T(149) = 4.2, p < .001), insurance (M_{hed} = 3.0, M_{ut} = 2.5, T(147) = 3.1, p < .01), and overestimation (M_{hed} = 3.8, M_{ut} = 2.7, T(125) = 6.8, p < .001) effects are significantly higher in the hedonic situation, in support of H_2, H_3, and H_4. There is no support for H_1 as there is no significant difference of the convenience effect between the two scenarios. Overall, the flat-rate bias is significantly higher in the hedonic context than in the utilitarian consumption situation (M_{hed} = 3.1, M_{ut} = 2.2, T(152) = 6.8, p < .001), in support of H_5.

	Hedonic		*Utilitarian*			
	M	*SE*	*M*	*SE*	*df*	*T*
Convenience	2.41	.10	2.40	.10	148	.12
Taxi-meter	3.37	.09	2.81	.10	149	4.22***
Insurance	2.98	.10	2.51	.11	147	3.10**
Overestimation	3.79	.09	2.70	.13	125	6.84***
Tariff choice	3.09	.09	2.16	.11	152	6.83***

$^{**}p < .01$, $^{***}p < .001$.

Table 15—Independent Samples T-Test between Hedonic and Utilitarian Dance Lessons Scenario

To understand the causes for this difference, the hedonic scenario must be compared with the hybrid, which reveals the impact of adding a utilitarian consumption goal on the flat-rate bias effects and flat-rate choice. Table 16 contains the results of independent samples T-tests comparing the two scenarios. Only the overestimation effect shows a significant difference between the two scenarios—all other flat-rate bias effects do not differ significantly across the scenarios. Thus, flat-rate bias does not increase significantly with greater utilitarian service perceptions.

	Hedonic		*Hybrid*			
	M	*SE*	*M*	*SE*	*df*	*T*
Convenience	2.41	.10	2.16	.10	146	-1.62
Taxi-meter	3.37	.09	3.39	.09	146	.30
Insurance	2.98	.10	3.13	.12	146	1.25
Overestimation	3.79	.09	4.08	.10	146	-.53*
Tariff choice	3.09	.09	3.09	.09	145	-.06

$^{*}p < .05$.

Table 16—Independent Samples T-Test between Hedonic and Hybrid Dance Lessons Scenario

Comparing the utilitarian with the hybrid scenario isolates the impact of the hedonic consumption goal. As shown in Table 17, all flat-rate bias effects despite the convenience effect are significantly higher when hedonism gets added to the scenario description. The flat-rate bias thus is significantly higher with greater hedonic service perceptions.

	Utilitarian		*Hybrid*			
	M	*SE*	*M*	*SE*	*df*	*T*
Convenience	2.16	.10	2.16	.10	125	1.36
Taxi-meter	3.39	.09	3.39	.09	125	-4.47***
Insurance	3.13	.12	3.13	.12	125	-4.19***
Overestimation	4.08	.10	4.08	.10	114	-8.91***
Tariff choice	3.09	.09	3.09	.09	124	-7.06***

$^{***}p < .001$.

Table 17—Independent Samples T-Test between Utilitarian and Hybrid Dance Lessons Scenario

To test whether the flat-rate bias effects fully mediate the impact of the consumption goals on flat-rate choice (H_6) multi-categorical mediation analysis gets used (Hayes & Preacher, 2011). Compared to the classical causal steps approach it has less strict assumptions due to the use of bootstrapping and allows for several mediators (in this context the flat-rate bias effects) and independent variables (hedonic and utilitarian) (Preacher & Hayes, 2008; Zhao, Lynch Jr., & Chen, 2010).

The categorical variable of the scenario type (hedonic, utilitarian, hybrid) acts as independent variable, the three flat-rate bias effects as mediators, and flat-rate choice as dependent variable. The *mediate* SPSS macro (Hayes & Preacher, 2011) generates two dummy variables representing the change from the hybrid scenario to the pure utilitarian ($Delta_{hed}$) and the pure hedonic scenario ($Delta_{ut}$). Thus $Delta_{hed}$ represents the impact of a change in the hedonic, and $Delta_{ut}$ the impact of a change in the utilitarian dimension.

Also these results (see Table 18) show significant effects of the hedonic dimension ($Delta_{hed}$) on the taxi-meter, the insurance, and the overestimation effects supporting hypotheses H_2, H_3 and H_4. There is no direct effect on flat-rate choice when flat-rate bias effects are included and controlled for in the model. The utilitarian dimension ($Delta_{ut}$) has neither a significant effect on flat-rate bias effects nor a significant direct nor indirect effect on flat-rate choice. Overall, there is a significant total effect of the hedonic dimension on flat-rate choice confirming hypothesis H_5. Using a bootstrap confidence interval of 95% there are indirect effects of the hedonic dimension on flat-rate choice via the taxi-meter, the insurance and the overestimation effects confirming hypothesis H_6. No indirect effects of the utilitarian dimension can be observed.

	Coefficient	*SE*	*T*
Total Effects Model: FR-Choice	*R^2 = .19*	*F = 25.76****	
Constant	3.06	.10	
$Delta_{hed}$	-.87	.14	-6.05***
$Delta_{ut}$	.03	.14	.19
Partial Model: Convenience Effect	*R^2 = .01*	*F = 2.43**	
Constant	2.14	.10	
$Delta_{hed}$	.27	.14	1.88
$Delta_{ut}$	.27	.14	1.96
Partial Model: Taxi-Meter Effect	*R^2 = .08*	*F = 9.56****	
Constant	3.35	.09	
$Delta_{hed}$	-.49	.13	-3.66***
$Delta_{ut}$	.02	.13	.16
Partial Model: Insurance Effect	*R^2 = .07*	*F = 8.22****	
Constant	3.15	.11	
$Delta_{hed}$	-.64	.16	-3.92***
$Delta_{ut}$	-.18	.15	-1.14
Partial Model: Overestimation Effect	*R^2 = .30*	*F = 45.24****	
Constant	4.07	.11	
$Delta_{hed}$	-1.41	.16	-8.96***
$Delta_{ut}$	-.28	.15	-1.90

	Coefficient	*SE*	*T*
Overall Model: Flat-Rate Choice	$R^2 = .41$	$F = 24.38$***	
Constant	.92	.29	
$Delta_{hed}$	-.24	.15	-1.64
$Delta_{ut}$	.16	.12	1.35
Convenience	-.11	.06	-1.80
Taxi-Meter	.20	.07	2.67**
Insurance	.21	.06	3.55***
Overestimation	.26	.06	4.37***
Omnibus Test of Direct Effect	$R^2 = .03$	$F = 4.62$*	
	Effect	*LL 95% CI*	*UL 95% CI*
Indirect Effects through Convenience			
$Delta_{hed}$	-.03	-.09	.01
$Delta_{ut}$	-.03	-.09	.01
Omnibus	-.01	-.01	.01
Indirect Effects through Taxi-Meter			
$Delta_{hed}$	-.10*	-.20	-.02
$Delta_{ut}$	.01	-.05	.06
Omnibus	.01*	.00	.04
Indirect Effects through Insurance			
$Delta_{hed}$	-.14*	-.27	-.04
$Delta_{ut}$	-.04	-.13	.02
Omnibus	.01*	.01	.04
Indirect Effects through Overestimation			
$Delta_{hed}$	-.36*	-.57	-.18
$Delta_{ut}$	-.07	-.16	.01
Omnibus	.07*	.03	.13

*$p < .05$, **$p < .01$, ***$p < .001$.
Notes: LL = lower limit, UL = upper limit, CI = confidence interval.

Table 18—Mediation Analysis for Dance Lessons Scenarios

3.2.5.4 Summary of Study 2

Study 2 confirms hypotheses H_2, H_3, H_4, and H_5 with two different analysis methodologies, namely T-tests and mediation analysis based on multiple linear regression models. The hypothesis H_1 predicting a stronger convenience effect in the hedonic context gets no support. Finally, the mediation analysis confirms H_6 predicting full mediation of the consumption goal impact by the flat-rate bias effects. Compared to Study 1, Study 2 has the advantage of leveraging the same service for the generation of the three consumption goal scenarios. As one could argue that dancing lessons are very polarizing, and the fact that the pure hedonic scenario shows high utilitarian consumption goals, the third study uses a thermal bath visit instead but maintains the advantages of hypothetical scenarios for a third person.

3.2.6 Study 3: Thermal Bath Visit Scenarios

3.2.6.1 Description of Experimental Setup and Sample

Study 3 was conducted online (see Appendix B) in autumn 2010 by a professional marketing research agency in a between subjects design. The sample of 298 respondents represented the overall German population (Statistisches Bundesamt, 2006) (see Table 19):

Criterion	*Value*	*Should %*	*Actual %*
Gender	Male	49%	47%
	Female	51%	53%
Age	15-25 years	17%	15%
	25-45 years	41%	42%
	45-65 years	41%	42%
Education (highest degree)	"Hauptschule"	47%	46%
	"Abitur"	40%	40%
	"Diplom oder höher"	13%	14%
Gross Household Income	< €1,500 per month	8%	7%
	€1,500 - €2,500 p.m.	35%	33%
	€2,501 - €3,500 p.m.	32%	34%
	> € 3,500 p.m.	25%	26%

Table 19—Socio-Demographic Quotas and Characteristics of Respondents for Study 3

Respondents were randomly told one of three hypothetical stories of a visit to a thermal bath by a person named Andrea (Bargh & Chartrand, 2000). For the hedonic story, Andrea visits the baths just for fun and to have a good time. In the utilitarian story, she needs the mineral water to relieve the pain of her rheumatism. Finally, in the hybrid version, Andrea enjoys the leisure time she spends at the baths but also believes the mineral water is good for her skin. In each case, a short descriptive text explained Andrea's consumption goal for her next thermal bath visit (see Table 20). The goal of this priming was to cause respondents put themselves in Andrea's shoes and subconsciously adopt her consumption goal (Kolb & Whishaw, 2003).

Scenario	*Scenario Description*
Hedonic	Andrea loves thermal baths. She finds the water slides thrilling, exciting, and fun; but she also enjoys the silence and relaxing in the hot water. However, sometimes she feels bad about it: It is neither useful nor necessary for her to go there. It's just for fun.
Utilitarian	For Andrea, thermal baths are not for fun or enjoyment. The thermal water is a really useful means to treat her rheumatism. Bathing in the hot water relieves her pain and thus effectively increases her wellbeing. Thermal baths are a very helpful medication for her.
Hybrid	Andrea has fun with the exciting and thrilling water slides. But she also enjoys the silence of relaxing in the hot water, which helps her forget about work. Furthermore, the minerals in the water are very effective for her to get clean skin.

Table 20—Description of Thermal Bath Visit Scenarios

For all scenarios, Andrea's past visits ranged from a minimum of two hours to an average of four to a maximum of six hours. The rates were €4 per hour or €16 for a day pass, in line with typical German thermal baths. Measurement Scale Validation and Manipulation Checks

3.2.6.2 Measurement Scale Validation and Manipulation Checks

Table 21 shows that the Exploratory and the Confirmatory Factor Analysis achieve good results for the Thermal Bath scenario.

Effect/Scale Item	*α* CITC	*EV* FL	*FR* SRW	*AVE* *IR*
Convenience	*.92*	*.86*	*.92*	*.79*
c1	.80	.91	.84	.71
c2	.86	.94	.92	.85
c3	.85	.93	.91	.83
Taxi-Meter	*.92*	*.77*	*.92*	*.71*
t1	.78	.86	.84	.71
t2	.80	.88	.80	.64
t3	.82	.89	.87	.76
t4	.87	.92	.93	.86
t5	.74	.83	.75	.56
Insurance	*.91*	*.74*	*.91*	*.66*
i1	.71	.80	.63	.40
i2	.73	.82	.66	.44
i3	.79	.88	.89	.79
i4	.85	.92	.95	.90
i5	.78	.87	.89	.79

Effect/Scale Item	*α* CITC	*EV* FL	*FR* SRW	*AVE* *IR*
Overestimation	*.96*	*.90*	*.97*	*.87*
o1	.87	.92	.90	.81
o2	.94	.97	.96	.92
o3	.93	.96	.95	.90
o4	.91	.95	.93	.86
Hedonic	*.98*	*.92*	*.97*	*.89*
h1	.95	.97	.98	.96
h2	.94	.96	.92	.85
h3	.90	.94	.92	.85
h4	.91	.94	.89	.79
h5	.96	.97	.99	.98
Utilitarian	*.92*	*.76*	*.92*	*.71*
u1	.85	.91	.91	.83
u2	.85	.91	.87	.76
u3	.85	.91	.90	.81
u4	.78	.86	.84	.71
u5	.66	.76	.67	.45
Fit Indices	*RMSEA*	χ^2/df	*TLI*	*CFI*
	.09	3.45	.91	.92

Notes: α = Cronbach's Alpha, CITC = Corrected Item-to-Total Correlation, *EV* = Explained Variance, FL = Factor Loading, *FR* = Factor Reliability, SRW = Standardized Regression Weight, *AVE* = Average Variance Extracted, IR = Indicator Reliability. KMO & Bartelett test met, Fornell/Larcker criterion met, correlation of two error terms.

Table 21—EFA & CFA for Thermal Bath Visit Scenarios

For the manipulation checks in Study 3, independent samples T-tests were used. As expected, the hedonic scenario is significantly less utilitarian than the hybrid one (M_{hed} = 3.07, SE_{hed} = .11, M_{hyb} = 4.09, SE_{hyb} = .07, T(152) = –7.61, $p <$ .001); there are no significant difference in hedonic perceptions between them (M_{hed} = 4.38, SE_{hed} = .08, M_{hyb} = 4.43, SE_{hyb} = .07, T(193) = –.46, $p > .05$). Accordingly, the utilitarian scenario is significantly less hedonic than the hybrid scenario (M_{ut} = 2.80, SE_{ut} = .13, M_{hyb} = 4.43, SE_{hyb} = .07, T(150) = –10.91, $p < .001$), but there is no significant difference in utilitarian perceptions between these two scenarios (M_{ut} = 4.07, SE_{ut} = .07, M_{hyb} = 4.09, SE_{hyb} = .07, T(206) = –.18, $p > .05$). Thus the priming was successful. The hedonic and utilitarian ratings of the three hypothetical scenarios can be found in Figure 9. Here, the respective distances between the hybrid and the hedonic/utilitarian scenarios are very similar.

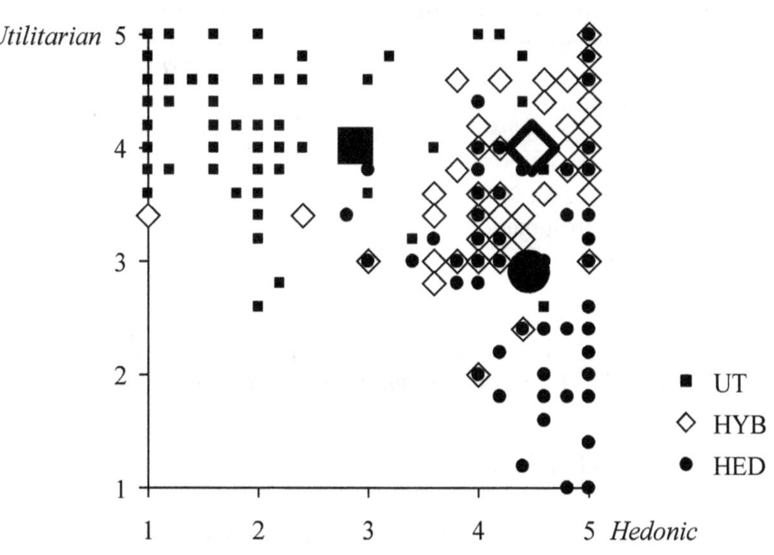

Figure 9—Hed/Ut Ratings of Thermal Bath Visit Scenarios

The linear regression model in Table 22 shows that two of the four flat-rate bias effects explain flat-rate choice to a substantial degree ($R^2 = .56$). The taxi-meter ($ß = .40$, $p < .001$) and overestimation ($ß = .38$, $p < .001$) effects have significant impacts on flat-rate choice. The insurance ($ß = .02$, $p > .05$) and the convenience ($ß = .02$, $p > .05$) effects do not contribute significantly to flat-rate choice in this setting though. This might be either due to the hypothetical scenario of making a decision for someone else (Johansson-Stenman, Carlsson, & Daruvala, 2002) or due to the nature of visiting a spa. The risk of over-usage is limited by the opening hours per day and therefore the need to insure against it is lower than for other services without such a natural limit. Furthermore, staying much more than 6 hours in a row might seem quite unlikely.

	B	*SE B*	*β*
Constant	.07	.16	
Convenience	.02	.04	.02
Taxi-meter	.38	.06	.40***
Insurance	.02	.07	.02
Overestimation	.32	.05	.38***
	$R^2 = .56$, F = 94***		

****p* < .001.

Notes: Dependent variable = tariff choice.

Table 22—Linear Regression for Thermal Bath Visit Scenarios

The logistic regression confirms these findings as shown in Table 23:

	B	*SE B*	*Exp(B)*
Constant	-8.73	1.17	
Convenience	.06	.22	1.06
Taxi-meter	1.33	.30	3.80***
Insurance	.18	.31	1.19
Overestimation	1.13	.25	3.10***
	Cox & Snell $R^2 = .47$		
	Nagelkerke $R^2 = .65$		

***$p < .001$.

Notes: Dependent variable = binary tariff choice.

Table 23—Logistic Regression for Thermal Bath Visit Scenarios

3.2.6.3 Empirical Findings

Comparing the hedonic with the utilitarian scenario with independent samples T-tests (see Table 24) reveals that the taxi-meter ($M_{hed} = 3.9$, $M_{ut} = 3.4$, $T(190) = 3.3$, $p < .001$), insurance ($M_{hed} = 3.8$, $M_{ut} = 3.3$, $T(190) = 3.4$, $p < .001$), and overestimation ($M_{hed} = 3.8$, $M_{ut} = 2.9$, $T(190) = 5.4$, $p < .001$) effects are significantly higher in the hedonic situation, in support of H_2, H_3, and H_4. The difference in the convenience effect between the two scenarios is not significant ($M_{hed} = 2.8$, $M_{ut} = 2.7$, $T(191) = .60$, $p > .05$) rejecting H_1. Overall, the flat-rate bias is significantly higher in the hedonic context than in the utilitarian consumption situation ($M_{hed} = 2.9$, $M_{ut} = 2.3$, $T(190) = 4.5$, $p < .001$), in support of H_5.

	Hedonic Scenario		*Utilitarian Scenario*			
	M	*SE*	*M*	*SE*	*df*	*T*
Convenience	2.82	.11	2.73	.10	191	.61
Taxi-meter	3.87	.10	3.40	.11	190	3.29***
Insurance	3.76	.09	3.30	.10	190	3.44***
Overestimation	3.75	.11	2.89	.12	190	5.35***
Tariff choice	2.91	.09	2.31	.10	190	4.48***

***$p < .001$.

Notes: Levene's test for equality of variances was taken into account.

Table 24—Independent Samples T-Test between Hedonic and Utilitarian Thermal Bath Visit Scenario

To understand the causes for this difference, one can compare the hedonic with the hybrid scenario, which reveals the impact of adding a utilitarian consumption goal on the flat-rate bias effects and flat-rate choice. Table 25 contains the results of independent samples T-tests comparing the two scenarios. None of the flat-rate bias effects differs significantly across the scenarios. Thus, flat-rate bias does not increase significantly with greater utilitarian service perceptions.

	Hedonic Scenario		*Hybrid Scenario*			
	M	*SE*	*M*	*SE*	*df*	*T*
Convenience	2.82	.11	3.10	.11	193	-1.77
Taxi-meter	3.87	.10	4.02	.09	193	-1.21
Insurance	3.76	.09	3.88	.08	193	-.97
Overestimation	3.75	.11	3.98	.09	193	-1.67
Tariff choice	2.91	.09	2.98	.08	193	-.58

$*p < .05$.
Notes: Levene's test for equality of variances was taken into account.

Table 25—Independent Samples T-Test between Hedonic and Hybrid Thermal Bath Visit Scenario

The comparison of the utilitarian with the hybrid scenario isolates the impact of the hedonic consumption goal. As shown in Table 26, all four flat-rate bias effects are all significantly higher when adding hedonism to the scenario description. The flat-rate bias thus is significantly higher with greater hedonic service perceptions.

	Utilitarian Scenario		*Hybrid Scenario*			
	M	*SE*	*M*	*SE*	*df*	*T*
Convenience	2.73	.10	3.10	.11	206	-2.54*
Taxi-meter	3.40	.11	4.02	.09	196	-4.56***
Insurance	3.30	.10	3.88	.08	206	-4.40***
Overestimation	2.89	.12	3.98	.09	186	-7.27***
Tariff choice	2.31	.10	2.98	.08	197	-5.19***

$*p < .05$, $***p < .001$.
Notes: Levene's test for equality of variances was taken into account.

Table 26—Independent Samples T-Test between Utilitarian and Hybrid Thermal Bath Visit Scenario

For testing the mediation hypothesis H_6, multi-categorical mediation analysis (Hayes & Preacher, 2011) gets applied. The scenario type (hedonic, utilitarian, hybrid) acts as categorical independent variable, the four flat-rate bias effects as mediators, and flat-rate choice as dependent variable. The results (see Table 27) show significant effects of the hedonic dimension ($\text{Delta}_{\text{hed}}$) on all flat-rate bias effects supporting hypotheses H_1, H_2, H_3, and H_4. There is no direct effect on flat-rate choice when flat-rate bias effects are included and controlled for in the model. The utilitarian dimension (Delta_{ut}) has neither a significant effect on flat-rate bias effects nor a significant direct nor indirect effect on flat-rate choice. Overall, there is a significant total effect of the hedonic dimension on flat-rate choice confirming hypothesis H_5. Using a bootstrap confidence interval of 95% one can see indirect effects of the hedonic dimension on flat-rate choice via the taxi-meter and the overestimation effects confirming hypothesis H_6. No indirect effects of the utilitarian dimension can be observed.

	Coefficient	*SE*	*T*
Total Effects Model: FR Choice	$R^2 = .10$	$F = 16.92$***	
Constant	2.98	.09	
$Delta_{hed}$	-.67	.13	-5.34***
$Delta_{ut}$	-.07	.13	-.54
Partial Model: Convenience Effect	$R^2 = .02$	$F = 3.43$*	
Constant	3.10	.10	
$Delta_{hed}$	-.37	.15	-2.52*
$Delta_{ut}$	-.28	.15	-1.84
Partial Model: Taxi-Meter Effect	$R^2 = .07$	$F = 11.78$***	
Constant	4.02	.09	
$Delta_{hed}$	-.63	.13	-4.69***
$Delta_{ut}$	-.16	.14	-1.13
Partial Model: Insurance Effect	$R^2 = .07$	$F = 11.44$***	
Constant	3.88	.09	
$Delta_{hed}$	-.58	.13	-4.56***
$Delta_{ut}$	-.12	.13	-.91
Partial Model: Overestimation Effect	$R^2 = .17$	$F = 30.44$***	
Constant	3.98	.10	
$Delta_{hed}$	-1.09	.15	-7.44***
$Delta_{ut}$	-.23	.15	-1.50
Overall Model: Flat-Rate Choice	$R^2 = .57$	$F = 63.16$***	
Constant	.13	.19	
$Delta_{hed}$	-.09	.10	-.94
$Delta_{ut}$	.07	.09	.71
Convenience	.02	.04	.60
Taxi-Meter	.38	.06	5.94***
Insurance	.02	.06	.30
Overestimation	.29	.05	5.70***
Omnibus Test of Direct Effect	$R^2 = .01$	$F = 1.31$	

	Effect	*LL 95% CI*	*UL 95% CI*
Indirect Effects through Convenience			
$Delta_{hed}$	-.01	-.04	.02
$Delta_{ut}$	-.01	-.03	.02
Omnibus	.00	-.00	.00
Indirect Effects through Taxi-Meter			
$Delta_{hed}$	-.24*	-.39	-.12
$Delta_{ut}$	-.06	-.16	.04
Omnibus	.03*	.01	.06
Indirect Effects through Insurance			
$Delta_{hed}$	-.01	-.10	.08
$Delta_{ut}$	-.00	-.03	.03
Omnibus	.00	-.01	.02
Indirect Effects through Overestimation			
$Delta_{hed}$	-.32*	-.49	-.18
$Delta_{ut}$	-.07	-.16	.01
Omnibus	-.05*	.02	.09

***$p < .001$, *$p < .05$.
Notes: LL = lower limit, UL = upper limit, CI = confidence interval.

Table 27—Mediation Analysis for Thermal Bath Visit Scenarios

3.2.6.4 Summary of Study 3

Study 3 confirms hypotheses H_2 to H_4 regarding the impact of the consumption goals on tariff choice. An impact on the convenience effect cannot be confirmed rejecting hypothesis H_1. Full mediation (H_6) gets confirmed for the taxi-meter and the overestimation effect. However, because respondents in Study 3 and 2 make the tariff choice for a third person, the results might have limited validity (Epley et al., 2002). Thus, the following studies pose the decision directly to the respondent.

3.2.7 Study 4: Hypothetical Thermal Bath Visit

3.2.7.1 Description of Experimental Setup and Sample

Study 4 was conducted together with Study 1 and 2 in a paper based questionnaire (see Appendix A) among marketing students. In the introductory text, students were presented a hypothetical thermal bath. The bath consists of several swimming pools, Jacuzzis, water slides, and saunas as well as steam baths for wellness and relaxation. Then they had to imagine that they were standing at the entrance of this bath and must decide for either tariff to enter: a day pass for €16 or a price of €4 per hour. As guidance they were told that they should assume the following past usage behavior—independent of their actual preferences: minimum 2 hours, on average 4 hours, and maximum 6 hours. Thus, the expected price of the hourly ticket matched the day pass exactly. Afterwards, tariff choice was recorded with the four point scale, as well as flat-rate bias effects and the individual consumption goals toward the visit.

3.2.7.2 Measurement Scale Validation and Manipulation Checks

To validate the measurement scales, EFA and CFA were performed on the data (see Table 28). The Exploratory Factor Analysis yields satisfactory results for all measurement constructs. The overall fit indices of the Confirmatory Factor Analysis are also adequate. However, the average variance extracted of the taxi-meter, the insurance, and the convenience effects, as well as the consumption goals are below the defined critical value of .50. Therefore, the taxi-meter and the insurance effect also miss the Fornell/Larcker ratio: -.06 for the taxi-meter effect scale in interaction with the insurance effect scale, and -.07 for the insurance effect scale interacting with the taxi-meter effect scale. Thus the reliability and discriminance validity of the scales with the reduced set of measurement items as used in the student sample seems to be lower than the full scales as used in the other studies.

Effect/Scale Item	*α* CITC	*EV* FL	*FR* SRW	*AVE* IR
Convenience	*.65*	*.74*	*.65*	*.48*
c1*	.48	.86	.70	.49
c2*	.48	.86	.69	.48
Taxi-Meter	*.73*	*.55*	*.60*	*.43*
t1*	.49	.72	.65	.42
t4*	.46	.78	.66	.44
Insurance	*.59*	*.71*	*.59*	*.42*
i1*	.42	.84	.63	.40
i2*	.42	.84	.67	.45
Overestimation	*.76*	*.81*	*.77*	*.62*
o1*	.61	.90	.86	.74
o2*	.61	.90	.71	.50
Hedonic	*.82*	*.60*	*.82*	*.49*
h1	.70	.85	.83	.69

Effect/Scale	α	*EV*	*FR*	*AVE*
Item	CITC	FL	SRW	IR
h2	.61	.73	.55	.30
h3	.62	.78	.76	.58
h4	.53	.67	.44	.19
h5	.66	.82	.83	.69
Utilitarian	*.82*	*.58*	*.82*	*.47*
u1	.56	.72	.65	.42
u2	.64	.78	.71	.50
u3	.67	.81	.73	.53
u4	.59	.75	.64	.41
u5	.60	.76	.69	.48
Fit Incides	*RMSEA*	χ^2/df	*TLI*	*CFI*
	.06	1.85	.90	.92

Notes: α = Cronbach's Alpha, CITC = Corrected Item-to-Total Correlation, *EV* = Explained Variance, FL = Factor Loading, *FR* = Factor Reliability, SRW = Standardized Regression Weight, *AVE* = Average Variance Extracted, IR = Indicator Reliability. KMO & Bartelett test met, Fornell/Larcker criterion met, correlation of two error terms.

[*] Reduced set of items to shorten survey.

Table 28—EFA & CFA for Hypothetical Thermal Bath Visit

The linear (see Table 29) and logistic (see Table 30) regression models proof the impact of flat-rate bias effects on tariff choice.

	B	*SE B*	β
Constant	.52	.22	
Convenience	-.04	.06	-.04
Taxi-meter	.38	.06	.36***
Insurance	.18	.06	.19**
Overestimation	.18	.05	.20**
	R^2 = .34, F = 32***		

$^{**}p < .01$, $^{***}p < .001$.

Notes: Dependent variable = tariff choice.

Table 29—Linear Regression for Hypothetical Thermal Bath Visit

	B	*SE B*	*Exp(B)*
Constant	-6.36	.99	
Convenience	-.28	.20	.76
Taxi-meter	1.16	.25	3.20***
Insurance	.65	.23	1.92**
Overestimation	.67	.18	1.96***
	Cox & Snell R^2 = .33		
	Nagelkerke R^2 = .44		

$^{**}p < .01$, $^{***}p < .001$.

Notes: Dependent variable = binary tariff choice.

Table 30—Logistic Regression for Hypothetical Thermal Bath Visit

Analyzing the consumption goals of the different respondents toward visiting the thermal baths it seems that there is quite some variance (see Figure 10). The average hedonic rating is at 3.71 with a standard deviation of .72. For the utilitarian dimension, the average is 2.50 and the standard deviation .75. This spread of consumption goals gets leveraged during the following analyses as predictor for flat-rate bias effects mediating tariff choice:

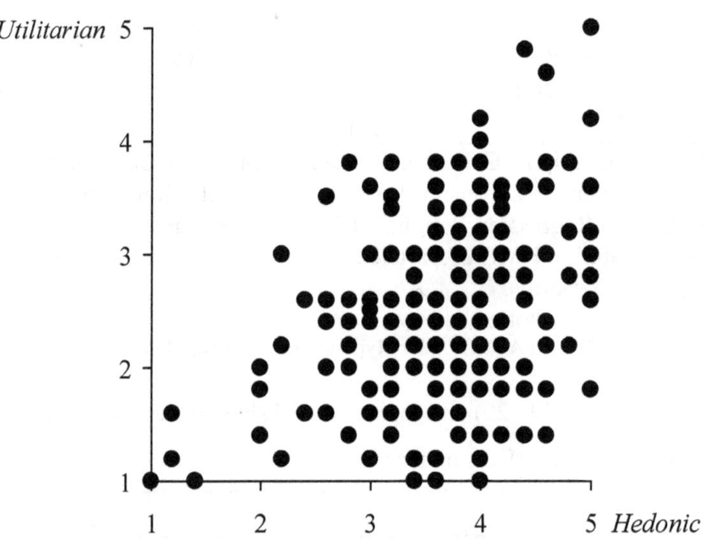

Figure 10—Hed/Ut Ratings of Hypothetical Thermal Bath Visit

3.2.7.3 Empirical Findings

To test hypothesis H_1 to H_6, the mediate SPSS macro (Hayes & Preacher, 2011) calculates several regression models (see Table 31) based on the consumption goals as two continuous independent variables, the flat-rate bias effects as mediators, and tariff choice as dependent variable. The partial models show that the taxi-meter and the overestimation effects get affected by hedonic consumption confirming H_2 and H_4. As the total effects model shows a significant impact of hedonic consumption goals on tariff choice, hypothesis H_5 gets also supported by the data. Finally, the taxi-meter and the overestimation effects fully mediate the impact of the hedonic consumption goals on tariff choice confirming hypothesis H_6.

	Coefficient	*SE*	*T*
Total Effects Model: Flat-Rate Choice	$R^2 = .03$	$F = 3.58*$	
Constant	1.95	.30	
$Delta_{hed}$	.21	.08	2.54*
$Delta_{ut}$	-.02	.08	-.23
Partial Model: Convenience Effect	$R^2 = .01$	$F = .96$	
Constant	2.31	.29	
$Delta_{hed}$	-.11	.08	-1.31
$Delta_{ut}$	.01	.08	.09
Partial Model: Taxi-Meter Effect	$R^2 = .09$	$F = 12.16***$	
Constant	1.84	.27	
$Delta_{hed}$	.32	.08	4.30***
$Delta_{ut}$	.04	.07	.53
Partial Model: Insurance Effect	$R^2 = .04$	$F = 5.10***$	
Constant	1.64	.30	
$Delta_{hed}$	.15	.08	1.78
$Delta_{ut}$	.14	.08	.08
Partial Model: Overestimation Effect	$R^2 = .09$	$F = 11.65***$	
Constant	1.85	.32	
$Delta_{hed}$	.33	.09	3.73***
$Delta_{ut}$	.11	.08	1.36
Overall Model: Flat-Rate Choice	$R^2 = .34$	$F = 20.48***$	
Constant	.69	.30	
$Delta_{hed}$	-.01	.07	-.16
$Delta_{ut}$	-.08	.07	-1.19
Convenience	-.05	.06	-.86
Taxi-Meter	.41	.07	6.07***
Insurance	.19	.06	2.98**
Overestimation	.17	.05	3.19**
Omnibus Test of Direct Effect	$R^2 = .01$	$F = .90$	

	Effect	*LL 95% CI*	*UL 95% CI*
Indirect Effects through Convenience			
$Delta_{hed}$	.01	-.01	.11
$Delta_{ut}$	-.00	-.02	.01
Omnibus	.00	-.00	.00
Indirect Effects through Taxi-Meter			
$Delta_{hed}$	.13*	.06	.21
$Delta_{ut}$	.02	-.05	.08
Omnibus	.03*	.01	.07
Indirect Effects through Insurance			
$Delta_{hed}$	.03	-.00	.07
$Delta_{ut}$	.03	-.00	.07
Omnibus	.01	-.00	.02

Indirect Effects through Overestimation			
$Delta_{hed}$	.06*	.01	.11
$Delta_{ut}$	.02	-.01	.06
Omnibus	.01*	.00	.04

$^{***}p < .001$, $^{**}p < .01$, $^{*}p < .05$.
Notes: LL = lower limit, UL = upper limit, CI = confidence interval.

Table 31—Mediation Analysis for Hypothetical Thermal Bath Visit

3.2.7.4 Summary of Study 4

Summarizing one can say that Study 4 supports hypotheses H_2 (taxi-meter effect), H_4 (overestimation effect), and H_5 (overall hedonic impact on flat-rate choice). Hypotheses H_1 and H_3 get no support. Furthermore, full mediation via the taxi-meter and the overestimation effects gets confirmed (H_6). Study 4 leveraged the natural variance of different individuals toward the same service. To increase external validity and ensure the generalization of the results, another Study using the same approach but with a different service follows.

3.2.8 Study 5: Hypothetical Energy Museum Visit

3.2.8.1 Description of Experimental Setup and Sample

Study 5 analyzes the natural variance of consumption goals across different respondents toward the same service. As the pretest shows, visiting a museum fulfills both hedonic and utilitarian consumption goals; a standard deviation of .88 for the hedonic and 1.2 for the utilitarian dimension also indicates sufficient natural variance in its consumption goals.

The marketing research agency Research Now conducted Study 5 online with a sample representative for the German population (see Appendix C) in summer 2011. 376 respondents had to imagine that they were going on a weekend trip to a new city, whose main attraction was an Energy Museum. A guidebook suggested that to visit the museum, people would need at least one hour, an average of three hours, and a maximum of five hours. The available rates were either €4 per hour or a day pass for €12 (i.e., average of three hours × €4). Again, respondents chose their preferred price plan on the four-point scale and explained their decision across the four flat-rate bias effect and the hed/ut scales. The socio-demographic criteria of the sample are shown in Table 32.

Criterion	*Value*	*Should %*	*Actual %*
Gender	Male	49%	49%
	Female	51%	51%
Age	15-25 years	17%	18%
	25-45 years	41%	40%
	45-65 years	41%	42%
Education (highest degree)	"Hauptschule"	47%	47%
	"Abitur"	40%	41%
	"Diplom oder höher"	13%	12%
Net Household Income	< €1,000 per month	10%	11%
	€1,000 - €1,500 p.m.	17%	16%
	€1,501 - €2,000 p.m.	19%	18%
	€2,001 - €2,500 p.m.	15%	16%
	€2,501 - €3,500 p.m.	12%	11%
	> € 3,500 p.m.	27%	28%

Table 32—Socio-Demographic Quotas and Characteristics of Study 5

The average hedonic and utilitarian ratings were quite balanced (M_{hed} = 3.46, M_{ut} = 3.19), with standard deviations of 1.01 (hedonic) and .99 (utilitarian). A scatter plot shows the individual answers along the hedonic and utilitarian dimensions (see Figure 11).

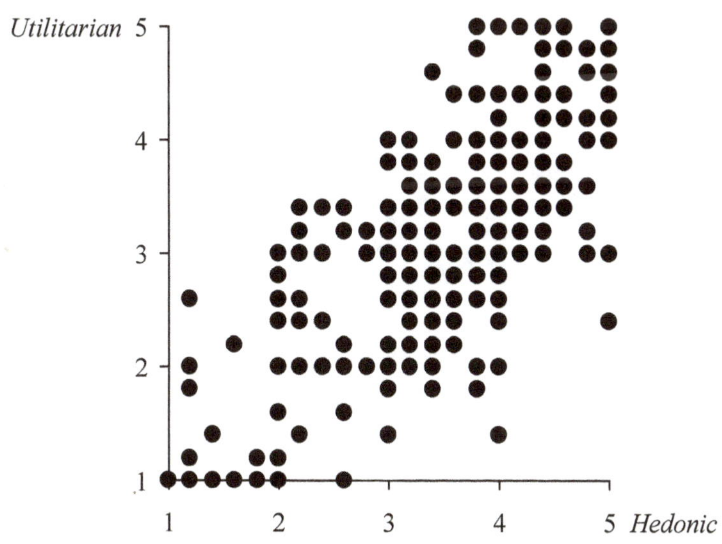

Figure 11—Hed/Ut Ratings of Hypothetical Energy Museum Visit

In this experiment, the hedonic and utilitarian dimensions seem to be quite collinear. Therefore, a test for multicollinearity has been performed. The tolerance value of .39 is larger than the critical value of .20; Thus, also the variance inflation factor of 2.56 is smaller than the critical value of 5 (O'Brien, 2007). Also the Condition Number of 12.80 (using the hedonic and the utilitarian dimension to explain flat-rate choice) is below the critical value of 30 (Grewal, Cote, & Baumgartner, 2004). Hence, multicollinearity seems to be not a critical problem.

3.2.8.2 Measurement Scale Validation and Manipulation Checks

Table 33 shows that the Exploratory and the Confirmatory Factor Analysis achieve good results for the Energy Museum visits. Only item i1 and i2 of the insurance effect scale do not achieve the desired level of indicator reliability which leads to a Fornell-Larcker ratio of -.05. All other criteria are adequately met.

Effect/Scale Item	*α* CITC	*EV* FL	*FR* SRW	*AVE* IR
Convenience	*.83*	*.74*	*.83*	*.62*
c1	.64	.84	.72	.52
c2	.69	.87	.80	.64
c3	.71	.88	.83	.69
Taxi-Meter	*.87*	*.66*	*.87*	*.58*
t1	.67	.79	.73	.53
t2	.68	.80	.71	.50
t3	.72	.83	.80	.64
t4	.70	.82	.78	.61
t5	.74	.84	.78	.61
Insurance	*.82*	*.60*	*.83*	*.52*
i1	.44	.58	.44	.19
i2	.60	.73	.60	.36
i3	.69	.84	.81	.66
i4	.75	.88	.88	.77
i5	.63	.80	.77	.59
Overestimation	*.92*	*.81*	*.92*	*.74*
o1	.83	.91	.89	.79
o2	.82	.90	.87	.76
o3	.82	.90	.86	.74
o4	.80	.89	.83	.69
Hedonic	*.94*	*.80*	*.94*	*.75*
h1	.85	.91	.88	.77
h2	.80	.87	.83	.69
h3	.81	.88	.85	.72
h4	.87	.92	.90	.81
h5	.84	.90	.87	.76

Effect/Scale Item	α CITC	*EV* FL	*FR* SRW	*AVE* IR
Utilitarian	*.94*	*.81*	*.94*	*.75*
u1	.85	.91	.90	.81
u2	.85	.91	.91	.83
u3	.85	.91	.87	.76
u4	.79	.86	.80	.64
u5	.74	.90	.86	.74
Fit Indices	*RMSEA*	χ^2/df	*TLI*	*CFI*
	.07	2.69	.92	.93

Notes: α = Cronbach's Alpha, CITC = Corrected Item-to-Total Correlation, *EV* = Explained Variance, FL = Factor Loading, *FR* = Factor Reliability, SRW = Standardized Regression Weight, *AVE* = Average Variance Extracted, IR = Indicator Reliability. KMO & Bartelett test met, Fornell/Larcker criterion met, correlation of two error terms.

Table 33—EFA & CFA for Hypothetical Energy Museum Visit

A linear regression model (see Table 34) shows that the taxi-meter and the overestimation effects explain a substantial portion of flat-rate choice (R^2 = .46). The insurance and the convenience effects instead do no influence tariff choice. The results get confirmed when forcing tariff choice to a binary decision (see Table 35).

	B	*SE B*	β
Constant	.18	.18	
Convenience	-.03	.04	-.03
Taxi-meter	.38	.05	.40***
Insurance	.06	.06	.05
Overestimation	.31	.04	.34***
	R^2 = .46, F = 78***		

***$p < .001$.

Notes: Dependent variable = tariff choice.

Table 34—Linear Regression for Hypothetical Energy Museum Visit

	B	*SE B*	*Exp(B)*
Constant	-9.17	1.11	
Convenience	-.01	.17	.99
Taxi-meter	1.50	.25	4.47***
Insurance	.17	.27	1.19
Overestimation	1.20	.20	3.31***
	Cox & Snell R^2 = .45		
	Nagelkerke R^2 = .61		

***$p < .001$.

Notes: Dependent variable = binary tariff choice.

Table 35—Logistic Regression for Hypothetical Energy Museum Visit

3.2.8.3 Empirical Findings

To test all hypotheses including mediation the mediate macro gets applied as in Study 4 (Hayes & Preacher, 2011). The hedonic and utilitarian ratings acted as independent variables using the whole range of the scale, the four flat-rate bias effects as mediators, and flat-rate choice as dependent variable.

There are significant effects of the hedonic dimension on the taxi-meter, the insurance, and the overestimation effect supporting hypotheses H_2, H_3, and H_4 (see Table 36). In contradiction with hypothesis H_1, the hedonic dimension does not increase the convenience effect. There is no direct effect of hedonic consumption goals on flat-rate choice when flat-rate bias effects are included and controlled for in the model. Interestingly, the utilitarian dimension has a significant effect on the insurance and the overestimation effect but at a lower significance level than the hedonic dimension. There is also no significant direct effect of utilitarian consumption goals on flat-rate choice when controlling for the flat-rate bias effects' impact. There is a significant total effect of the hedonic dimension on flat-rate choice confirming hypothesis H_5 yet no significant total effect of the utilitarian dimension on flat-rate choice. Using a bootstrap confidence interval of 95%, indirect effects of the hedonic dimension on flat-rate choice via the taxi-meter and the overestimation effects can be seen confirming hypothesis H_6. Also there is an indirect effect of the utilitarian dimension on flat-rate choice via the overestimation effect. The size of the utilitarian effect (.04) however is less than one third the size of the hedonic effect (.15).

	Coefficient	*SE*	*T*
Total Effects Model: Flat-Rate Choice	*$R^2 = .20$*	*$F = 46.99$****	
Constant	1.17	.16	
$Delta_{hed}$	.41	.07	5.90***
$Delta_{ut}$	.01	.07	.20
Partial Model: Convenience Effect	*$R^2 = .01$*	*$F = 1.92$*	
Constant	2.54	.20	
$Delta_{hed}$	.01	.08	.07
$Delta_{ut}$	.10	.09	1.17
Partial Model: Taxi-Meter Effect	*$R^2 = .20$*	*$F = 45.40$****	
Constant	2.13	.17	
$Delta_{hed}$	.35	.07	4.80***
$Delta_{ut}$	.10	.07	1.39

	Coefficient	*SE*	*T*
Partial Model: Insurance Effect	$R^2 = .21$	$F = 48.67$***	
Constant	2.37	.14	
$Delta_{hed}$	.23	.06	3.92***
$Delta_{ut}$	.16	.06	2.59**
Partial Model: Overestimation Effect	$R^2 = .42$	$F=136.95$***	
Constant	.72	.15	
$Delta_{hed}$	.54	.07	8.35***
$Delta_{ut}$	.16	.07	2.40*
Overall Model: Flat-Rate Choice	$R^2 = .46$	$F = 52.56$***	
Constant	.12	.19	
$Delta_{hed}$	.12	.06	1.89
$Delta_{ut}$	-.07	.06	-1.24
Convenience	-.03	.04	-.69
Taxi-Meter	.38	.05	7.02***
Insurance	.05	.06	.81
Overestimation	.28	.06	5.42***
Omnibus Test of Direct Effect	$R^2 = .01$	$F = 1.78$	

	Effect	*LL 95% CI*	*UL 95% CI*
Indirect Effects through Convenience			
$Delta_{hed}$	-.00	-.01	.01
$Delta_{ut}$	-.00	-.02	.01
Omnibus	-.00	-.00	.00
Indirect Effects through Taxi-Meter			
$Delta_{hed}$	.13*	.07	.20
$Delta_{ut}$	.04	-.02	.09
Omnibus	.07*	.04	.11
Indirect Effects through Insurance			
$Delta_{hed}$	.01	-.02	.05
$Delta_{ut}$	.01	-.01	.04
Omnibus	.01	-.02	.04
Indirect Effects through Overestimation			
$Delta_{hed}$	.15*	.09	.22
$Delta_{ut}$	.04*	.01	.09
Omnibus	.12*	.07	.17

***$p < .001$, *$p < .05$.
Notes: LL = lower limit, UL = upper limit, CI = confidence interval.

Table 36—Mediation Analysis for Hypothetical Energy Museum Visit

3.2.8.4 Summary of Study 5

Study 5 also shows that hedonic consumption goals drive flat-rate bias. In this context, the taxi-meter and the overestimation effects are the mediators of the consumption goals' impact. Thus, five studies consistently point into the same direction drawing to the conclusion that the hedonic not utilitarian consumption goals influence tariff choice in favor of flat-rates. This lets conclude that service providers should increase the hedonic consumption goals in order to increase the flat-rate bias of their customers. To see if this has also any effects on the willingness-to-pay, the sixth study investigates this question.

3.2.9 Study 6: Advertising Primed Hypothetical Thermal Bath Visit

3.2.9.1 Description of Experimental Setup and Sample

In order to find out if stressing hedonic aspects of a service to increase flat-rate bias also increases the willingness to pay (H_7), Study 6 measures the willingness to pay for three different service advertisements. All advertisements feature a thermal bath visit which has been proven in the pretest to be ambiguous regarding the consumption goals. The advertisements foster either the hedonic aspects of visiting a thermal bath, the utilitarian, or both at the same time. It was taken care that despite fostering different consumption goals the central service offering remains the same. Otherwise, ulterior dominant features of the offering might distort the choice situation (Carson et al., 1994; Krieger & Green, 1991).

In a between subject design, 194 respondents were assigned randomly to one of the three experimental conditions. In each condition respondents first saw the hypothetical advertisement for the thermal bath followed by a short instruction to carefully watch the advertisement and to focus on this hypothetical thermal bath and not any other known thermal bath when answering the questions. Next, respondents had to state their intended willingness to pay for a day pass with an open ended question (Miller et al., 2011). Furthermore, the preference between flat-rate and pay-per-use pricing was also asked for to compare the results with the previous studies. Subsequently, the hedonic and utilitarian consumption goals were measured using the hed/ut scales (K. E. Voss et al., 2003). Finally, the attitude towards the ad was captured with a 5-item measurement scale (Biehal et al., 1992) to make sure potential differences in the willingness to pay are not driven by the advertisement but by the consumption goals. The questionnaire can be found in Appendix D.

3.2.9.2 Manipulation Checks

Independent samples T-tests show that not all respondents perceived the primed advertisements as intended. The hedonic scenario differs from the hybrid in the hedonic (M_{hed} = 3.50, SE_{hed} = .08, M_{hyb} = 3.23, SE_{hyb} = .09, T(119) = 2.20, $p <$ .05), not the utilitarian rating (M_{hed} = 2.51, SE_{hed} = .12, M_{hyb} = 2.58, SE_{hyb} = .12, T(119) = -.39, p = n.s.). The utilitarian does not differ at all from the hybrid scenario (hedonic dimension: M_{ut} = 2.99, SE_{ut} = .09, M_{hyb} = 3.23, SE_{hyb} = .09, T(125) = -1.89, p = n.s., utilitarian dimension: M_{ut} = 2.68, SE_{ut} = .10, M_{hyb} = 2.58, SE_{hyb} = .12, T(125) = .63, p = n.s.). Under these circumstances, no conclusion on the willingness to pay can be made.

However, the goal of this study is not to proof *how* pure hedonic or pure utilitarian advertisement can be designed. This would be a separate topic in the field of advertising research. The goal is to show that if (assuming well designed advertisement) respondents perceive a service advertisement as more hedonic or utilitarian this has no impact on the willingness to pay. Thus, filtering out those respondents where priming through the advertisements did not work properly shall solve this problem.

The algorithm used to filter out the respective respondents is the following. In the hedonic scenario, respondents perceived the advertisement as "pure" hedonic if the hedonic rating is higher than the utilitarian; vice versa for the utilitarian scenario. The average hedonic and utilitarian rating in the hybrid scenario is M_{hed} = 3.23, and M_{ut} = 2.58. Thus, there is a delta of .6 between the two means. Therefore this .6 delta must be considered when filtering out the respondents in the hedonic and the utilitarian scenario; hence for the hedonic context only respondents with hedonic ratings higher than utilitarian ratings plus .6 are included in the analysis; and for the utilitarian context only respondents with utilitarian ratings higher than hedonic ratings minus .6 will be looked at. This reduces the sample size to 136.

3.2.9.3 Empirical Findings

Now, the hedonic and utilitarian ratings between the scenarios differ as intended. Despite significant higher hedonic and lower utilitarian consumption goal ratings between the hedonic and the utilitarian scenario, the willingness to pay of respondents does not differ (see Table 37) rejecting hypothesis H_7. In line with the previous studies, flat-rate bias is significantly higher for the hedonic scenario underlining the robustness of the findings. There is no significant difference between the two scenarios regarding the attitude toward the ad controlling for the potential alternative explanation.

	HED Ad (n=39)		*UT Ad (n=43)*			
	M	*SE*	*M*	*SE*	*df*	*T*
WTP for Flat-Rate	11.8	.64	11.9	.91	74	-.12
Flat-Rate Choice	2.7	.12	2.3	.14	80	2.1*
Hedonic	3.6	.11	2.7	.11	80	6.0***
Utilitarian	2.0	.12	2.9	.14	80	-5.0***
Attitude Toward Ad	2.3	.12	2.1	.10	80	.95

*$p < .05$, ***$p < .001$.

Notes: Levene's test for equality of variances was taken into account.

Table 37—Independent Samples T-Test between Hedonic and Utilitarian Advertisement

Comparing the hybrid scenario with the pure hedonic and the pure utilitarian also shows no significant difference in the willingness to pay (see Table 38 and Table 39).

	HED Ad (n=39)		*HYB Ad (n=54)*			
	M	*SE*	*M*	*SE*	*df*	*T*
WTP for Flat-Rate	11.8	.64	12.7	.75	91	-.92
Flat-Rate Choice	2.7	.12	2.6	.11	91	.83
Hedonic	3.6	.11	3.2	.09	91	2.8**
Utilitarian	2.0	.12	2.6	.12	91	-3.4***
Attitude Toward Ad	2.3	.12	2.2	.09	91	.72

**$p < .01$, ***$p < .001$.

Notes: Levene's test for equality of variances was taken into account.

Table 38—Independent Samples T-Test between Hedonic and Hybrid Advertisement

	UT Ad (n=43)		*HYB Ad (n=54)*			
	M	*SE*	*M*	*SE*	*df*	*T*
WTP for Flat-Rate	11.9	.91	12.7	.75	95	-.70
Flat-Rate Choice	2.3	.14	2.6	.11	95	-1.5
Hedonic	2.7	.11	3.2	.09	95	-3.9***
Utilitarian	2.9	.14	2.6	.12	95	2.0*
Attitude Toward Ad	2.1	.10	2.2	.09	95	-.3

*$p < .05$, ***$p < .001$.

Notes: Levene's test for equality of variances was taken into account.

Table 39—Independent Samples T-Test between Utilitarian and Hybrid Advertisement

3.2.9.4 Summary of Study 6

Study 6 shows that the "hedonization" of services to increase flat-rate bias does not increase customers' willingness to pay. But it also does not lead to a decrease as negative side effect which other research might make one to expect (Shiv et al., 2005). This is an important finding as a potential negative impact on the willingness to pay might compensate the benefits of increased flat-rate bias. Still, the "hedonization" increases flat-rate bias which has positive implications for the service providers.

3.3 Discussion

3.3.1 Summary of Studies 1 to 6

The first five studies confirm the current state of research that the taxi-meter, the insurance, and the overestimation but not the convenience effects lead to flat-rate bias. Furthermore, those three flat-rate bias effects are stronger in a hedonic context compared to a utilitarian supporting H_2, H_3, and H_4, but not the convenience effect contradicting H_1. As a result from the stronger flat-rate bias effects in the hedonic context, also flat-rate bias is stronger in a hedonic setting confirming hypothesis H_5. Specifically, the flat-rate bias effects fully mediate the impact of the consumption goals on tariff choice (H_6).

Finally, study 6 shows that, although the hedonic consumption goal impacts the decision between pay-per-use and flat-rate pricing, there is no impact on the general willingness to pay for a service rejecting hypothesis H_7. A summary of all hypotheses test results answering research question RQ_1 can be found in Table 40.

Hypothesis	*Study 1*	*Study 2*	*Study 3*	*Study 4*	*Study 5*	*Study 6*
RQ_1: Do service consumption goals affect FRB effects and subsequently FRB?						
Convenience Effect						
Impact on flat-rate bias?	Yes	No	No**	No	No	-
H_1: Hedonic impact stronger than utilitarian?	✓	×	×	×	×	
Taxi-Meter Effect						
Impact on flat-rate bias?	Yes	Yes	Yes	Yes	Yes	-
H_2: Hedonic impact stronger than utilitarian?	✓	✓	✓	✓	✓	
Insurance Effect						
Impact on flat-rate bias?	Yes	Yes	No	Yes	No	-
H_3: Hedonic impact stronger than utilitarian?	✓	✓	✓	×	✓	
Overestimation Effect						
Impact on flat-rate bias?	Yes*	Yes	Yes	Yes	Yes	-
H_4: Hedonic impact stronger than utilitarian?	✓	✓	✓	✓	✓	
Flat-Rate Bias						
H_5: Hedonic impact stronger than utilitarian?	✓	✓	✓	✓	✓	-
Mediation						
H_6: Flat-rate bias effects as full mediators	-	✓[1]	✓[2]	✓[2]	✓[2]	-
Willingness-to-Pay						
H_7: Impact of hedonic consumption goals on willingness-to-pay	-	- - - -				×

Notes: – = not applicable, ✓ = hypothesis confirmed, × = hypothesis not confirmed. *No for Public Transportation, **Confirmed by T-test but not by mediation analysis. [1]despite convenience effect, [2]despite convenience and insurance effect.

Table 40—Overview of Hypotheses H_1 to H_7 Test Results

As a conclusion, the research findings reveal that flat-rate bias differs for services depending on the underlying consumption goals: Consuming services to attain hedonic gratification leads to a significantly higher flat-rate bias than using services to fulfill utilitarian needs. The more hedonic a service, the higher the taxi-meter, insurance, and overestimation effects and the stronger flat-rate bias. Thus consumption goals have a significant influence on service tariff choice of customers. Service providers can predict by the nature of their service offerings if the introduction of a flat-rate likely results in a high share of flat-rate bias customers who contribute to a higher profitability. Also the findings indicate that service providers can increase the flat-rate bias of their customers by promoting and designing a hedonic consumption experience.

3.3.2 Theoretical Implications

The findings contribute to flat-rate bias research in at least three ways. First, this is the only research study to systematically compare flat-rate biases across services. In existing studies, it is hard to compare the flat-rate bias levels because they apply different methodologies; this research adopts consistent measures of flat-rate bias and measures all causes for all services to support a direct comparison. The results show that the causes of flat-rate bias, as well as flat-rate bias itself, depend on the service type. Consumers exhibit a different degree of flat-rate bias for different types of services, such as public transportation versus amusement parks. This finding confirms the initial observation that flat-rate bias varies across existing studies because they consider different services. So far, the conceptual model of flat-rate bias only incorporates consumer related predictors (four psychological effects). It should be extended by service related elements for a more differentiated view.

Second, this research specifies that the service specific consumption goals explain a substantial part of this variance. The flat-rate bias is stronger in hedonic than in utilitarian contexts, and the individual flat-rate bias effects reveal the causes for this hedonic influence on flat-rate choice. The findings show that three flat-rate bias effects are stronger in hedonic than in utilitarian contexts. The taxi-meter effect is based on mental accounting (Heath & Soll, 1996; Kivetz, 1999; Shefrin & Thaler, 1992; Thaler, 1985) and prospect theory (Kahneman & Tversky, 1979) as part of behavioral decision research (Simonson et al., 2001). The stronger taxi-meter effect in the hedonic context implies that the relevance of behavioral decision theory is higher in a hedonic compared to a utilitarian context. The insurance effect is driven by the option value (Kridel et al., 1993) a customer assigns to the possibility of consuming more in the future. This option value seems to be higher in a hedonic context than in a utilitarian confirming Chitturi et al. (2007) who claim that if the desired level of consumption is met or exceeded, consumers value hedonic attributes more than utilitarian attributes. The overestimation steams from wishful thinking (Einhorn & Hogarth, 1986) which seems to be more relevant for hedonic than for utilitarian consumption. Associative imagery (Khan et al., 2004) also seems to be stronger in a hedonic context and leads to a less rational decision mode (Kahneman & Frederick, 2002) confirming the relevance of Paraducci's range frequency model (Nunes, 2000) explaining peoples' way of making usage predictions. The overall results might therefore potentially explain why public transportation is the only service, in a series of price plan choice experiments by Prelec and Loewenstein (1998), to display a flat-rate preference far below average as it is pure utilitarian. Only the convenience effect does not get affected by hedonic consumption goals in the majority of studies. This could mean that the emotional decision mode of hedonic consumption (Khan et al., 2004) still allows for rational pay-per-use calculations. Especially since the calculations are not extremely complicated and thus transaction costs are considerably low. Or it could be due to the fact that the convenience effect does not contribute to flat-rate choice (see discussion below).

Third, the results support Lambrecht and Skiera's (2006) findings that the taxi-meter, insurance, and overestimation effects but not the convenience effect lead to flat-rate biases. The convenience effect only leads to flat-rate bias in the first study comparing public transportation with amusement parks. This makes sense as those two services show a specifically high difference in the transaction costs (payment process) between the two tariffs (Nunes, 2000). Stamping the metro ticket for every ride or pulling out the wallet to pay for every amusement park fun ride means a lot of additional manual effort compared to the respective day passes. For public transportation, the day pass means that respondents have to stamp their ticket only once and then can just use the subway system without any further effort as access to the subway in Germany is not guarded by gates. The admission relies on the honesty of the user together with random ticket controls during the rides. Thus, a day pass leads to significantly increased convenience and lowers transaction costs; same for amusement parks where pay-per-ride means a manual payment for every ride as compared to a one time transaction at the beginning or the end. Thus, in contexts, where the flat-rate not only saves time in the tariff decision process but also lowers transaction costs during actual usage like for example with a more efficient payment process, the convenience effect seems to be a relevant driver of flat-rate bias. In all the other situations where payment is handled automatically and thus there is no difference in the transaction costs, the convenience effect only covers the tariff decision process. It seems—in line with the findings of Lambrecht and Skiera (2006) where payment was based on a monthly bill—not to be a decisive driver of flat-rate bias in such situations. Flat-rate bias theory hence should continue to incorporate the convenience effect but must cover the transaction costs of future payments besides the decision process more explicitly. The measurement scale of the convenience effect should be extended accordingly. Potential items could include: "The flat-rate is very convenient for me because it means less payment hassle", "I like the automated payment mechanism of the flat-rate as it saves me time". If those aspects would be covered better by the measurement construct, maybe hedonic consumption goals would also influence the convenience effect more consistently. The taxi-meter effect contributes to flat-rate choice in all five studies making it a very robust driver of flat-rate bias and confirming the relevance of mental account (Heath & Soll, 1996; Kivetz, 1999; Shefrin & Thaler, 1992; Thaler, 1985), prospect (Kahneman & Tversky, 1979), and guilt and justification theory (Okada, 2005). The insurance effect contributes to flat-rate choice in all studies despite study 3 and 5—the thermal bath and energy museum visits. Study 3 takes up the perspective of a third person where respondents have the challenge to put themselves into the shoes of that person and thus potentially less realistically evaluate the situation. Together with the fact that thermal bath visits are limited by the opening hours lowering the risk of unexpectedly high costs, this might explain why there is no significant impact of the insurance effect on flat-rate bias. For the energy museum visit in study 5 also the measurement of time as consumption unit with a natural limitation by the opening hours might explain the lack of influence of the insurance effect on flat-rate bias. This is in line with risk aversion theory (Miravete, 2000; Nunes, 2000; Train, 1991) predicting less need for insurance if risks are low. Overestimation leads to flat-rate choice in all studies despite the public transportation scenario in the first study. A reason for this might be that respondents were very familiar with public transportation and therefore better recalled past usage information. This could mean that Paraducci's range frequency theory (Nunes, 2000) depends on the familiarity of a user with a service when making usage predictions.

The findings also contribute to behavioral decision research. Prior research has analyzed the impact of consumption goals in various contexts, such as product design (e.g., Gill, 2008), product evaluations (e.g., Okada, 2005), or product choice (e.g., Maslow, 1968); and in various conditions, such as winning prizes versus earning rewards for hard work (e.g., O'Curry & Strahilevitz, 2001). The results show, for the first time, that consumption goals also affect tariff choice for services. Hedonic consumption motives cause customers to show a stronger flat-rate bias. The more hedonic the consumption goals, the less standard economic theory explains consumer behavior with regard to price plan choices for services. Furthermore, the results of the pretest identifying services for the tariff choice experiments support the notion that hedonic and utilitarian consumption goals are not two ends of a continuum but rather independent (K. E. Voss et al., 2003) as services have been found for various hedonic-utilitarian combinations (see Figure 6).

The findings are not limited to tariff choice though; they also contribute to general pricing research. Because flat-rate bias implies a relative preference for fixed versus variable costs, the findings also might apply to decisions between purchasing and leasing or renting. For example, a stronger preference for purchase is expected if a consumer considers a hedonic sports cars rather than a utilitarian minivan. Buying the car minimizes constant reminders of spending on hedonism (i.e., guilt and justification theory, part of the taxi-meter effect). Customers even might prefer buying hedonic cars for a higher price than they would pay if they were to rent or lease them. In contrast, for utilitarian cars such as minivans, consumers likely prefer to calculate the expected overall cost and choose the more economical option.

In contrast to the notion of Wakefield and Inman (2003), price sensitivity reflected by the willingness to pay does not seem to be higher for hedonic consumption. This effect might be compensated by the negative impact of hedonic consumption goals on the perceived price worthiness as predicted by Shif, Carmon and Ariely (2005).

3.3.3 Managerial Implications

Service providers can exploit such consumer behavior to increase their profits. Companies benefit from constant and predictable revenues of flat-rates. With a flat-rate bias, those revenues are higher and more profitable than the respective pay-per-use revenues would be. Still, customers enjoy consumption with no thought for the pain of paying and protection from bill shocks. Lambrecht and Skiera (2006) even claim that a flat-rate bias has no negative impact on customer churn, so flat-rates offer a universally beneficial rate. Service providers should attempt to increase the share of customers using flat-rates and maximize the prices of flat-rate offers.

To do so, service providers might trigger flat-rate bias effects in their communication (Lambrecht & Skiera, 2006) and/or "hedonize" their services (i.e., increase their hedonic perceptions). When customers perceive the service as more hedonic, the flat-rate bias effects become stronger, and customers prefer the flat-rate more. To increase hedonic perceptions, service providers must ensure the service consumption is a hedonic experience. If advertising promotes hedonic experience that is not met by the service delivery customers might get disappointed. Following Bitner (1993) there are three areas to cover determining the consumption experience: people, processes, and physical evidence. Selecting the right employees who enjoy their jobs is fundamental to transfer this enjoyment to customers. Further training staff to deliver "service with a smile" can change customer moods and make them perceive the service as more hedonic (Pugh, 2001). Designing the service delivery, providers should make sure that the process itself is a hedonic experience. Not only the utilitarian outcome counts, also the process of getting there is important following the notion that "the journey is the reward". In the luxury cars' segment for example, more and more automotive companies invite customers to an "open" production facility where they receive their newly bought car. The hand-over is designed as a ceremonial event with a short visit of the production facility, a handshake from an engineer and a glass of sparkling wine making the purchase a hedonic experience. Other examples are online tools. For instance, booking a flight with modern airlines, customers can self-select their seat on the screen viewing a small model of the aircraft. Although it is a simple utilitarian booking procedure, the tool is designed in a way to make the booking process a hedonic experience. Furthermore, the physical environment can enhance and foster the hedonic experience (Hightower, Brady, & Baker, 2002). During a flight, for example, in-flight entertainment systems make customers forget about (waiting) time to get from A to B. In short intervals, food and drinks are served further making the journey a hedonic experience. In retailing, new technologies like RFID will enable hedonic customer shopping experience in store environments (Uhrich, Sandner, Resatsch, Leimeister, & Krcmar, 2008). Leveraging those means to design hedonic customer journeys, conduct sensory design, and implement a dramatic structure of the service delivery process seems promising to successfully achieve a hedonic customer experience (Zomerdijk & Voss, 2009).

In order to make customers purchase services and chose flat-rates, providers first can advertise this hedonic experience to evoke the respective expectations (Deliza & MacFie, 1996). Instead of highlighting rational and quantitative benefits of the service, they should focus on the enjoyment derived from unlimited consumption. Describing their offer, service managers could make use of the vocabulary used in the hed/ut scale by Voss, Spangenberg, and Grohmann (2003). For example, they could highlight the *fun* of using their service. They can describe the service experience as either *exciting* and *thrilling*, or *delightful* and *enjoyable*—depending on the nature of the service. Those adjectives shall help trigger the hedonic service perception of subjects and subsequently flat-rate bias. To increase credibility, testimonials can be used to underline those characteristics with statements from existing customers. Emotional images reflecting the hedonic experience strengthen this effect.

3.3.4 Limitations and Further Research

This research has various limitations that suggest topics for further research. First, the findings are based on stated preferences in experimental settings. Real-life behavior sometimes differs from stated preferences. Everything was tried to make the choice tasks as realistic as possible (e.g., matching real prices, historic usage information, providing detailed scenario descriptions), but data on actual behavior would provide better external validity. Especially for the overestimation effect, an analysis of transactional data is essential, because a scale can only approximate overestimation. Thus a necessary next step is to validate the findings with transactional data about actual tariff choice.

Second, the recommendation to managers is to increase the hedonic perceptions of their services to foster flat-rate bias. Additional research could investigate in more detail how to increase the hedonic perception of services. A series of experiments might compare the impact of various measures (e.g., different forms of advertising) on hedonic service perceptions, and thus eventually on flat-rate bias effects and the flat-rate bias. A differentiation based on the nature of the service (hedonic versus utilitarian) could confirm if the "hedonization" works for all kinds of services. Gill (2008), for example, shows that utilitarian base products benefit more from hedonic add-ons than from utilitarian add-ons, which suggests that a flat-rate bias also might increase through the hedonic priming of pure utilitarian services. Similarly, Hill, Blodgett, Baer and Wakefield (2004) found out that advertising with visualization works for both, hedonic and utilitarian services. Thereby, potential negative side effects of the "hedonization" should be considered. Although no negative effect on the willingness to pay was found, further aspects like a potential impact on the value proposition or the target group of the service provider should be investigated. Especially if a service is pure utilitarian, adding hedonic consumption goals might change the value proposition and thus the service itself.

Third, the pretest used six criteria to ensure *ceteris paribus* conditions. Further research should determine if and how much these factors influence flat-rate bias. Such detail could give managers additional tools for increasing the flat-rate bias among consumers.

Fourth, all studies used the framework of Lambrecht and Skiera (2006) focusing on the convenience, taxi-meter, insurance, and overestimation effects as causes of flat-rate bias. As shown before, the convenience effect measurement scale should be extended to cover the transaction costs of the payment process. Furthermore, there might be other causes as well such as a "flexibility effect" favoring pay-per-use bias. Future research on flat-rate bias should consider such an effect or could have a closer look at the convenience effect. In this context it was rarely significant but in other contexts with more impact of transaction costs it could get a relevant cause of flat-rate bias.

4 Impact of Competitive Position on Flat-Rate Bias Consequences[3]

4.1 Hypotheses Development

4.1.1 Relevance of Flat-Rate Bias Consequences

Based on the findings of the first six studies, managers are advised to actively increase flat-rate bias through the "hedonization" of services. But the question is whether this is sustainable? If flat-rate bias has negative consequences on customer loyalty, increasing it through "hedonization" is not a sustainable means. So far, only one study analyzes the consequences of flat-rate bias finding no negative consequences on the Customer Lifetime Value (Lambrecht & Skiera, 2006). But it has several limitations and contradicts general research on tariff choice (see chapter 1.1.2). Therefore, this chapter re-investigates the consequences of flat-rate bias: (RQ_2) Does flat-rate bias increase tariff switching and customer churn, and (RQ_3) does the competitive position of a service provider moderate flat-rate bias consequences (i.e., churn and switching)?

4.1.2 Impact of Flat-Rate Bias on Switching

Following economic theory, customers are rationally acting individuals who strive to maximize their financial benefits (Brown & Sibley, 1986). Customers should choose the tariff that minimizes the expected costs and maximizes their expected utility. This means choosing the tariff i with the probability p_i so that $p_i * u(i)$ is maximized (Swalm, 1966). As the utility depends on the assumed future usage behavior, tariff choice is a decision under uncertainty. Under uncertainty, human decision-making is often only rational by intention. In practice, decisions often turn out to be wrong from an economical point of view violating rational choice theory (Allais, 1953). Once customers realize that their assumptions were wrong, they should—following economic theory—reassess their decision and switch their tariff to the right calling plan (Khan et al., 2004). Thus, similar to the findings of Lambrecht and Skiera (2006), it is expected:

[3] This chapter is based on joint research with Felix Frank.

H_{8a} Customers with flat-rate bias have higher switching rates than customers without flat-rate bias.

Behavioral decision researchers argue that consumer decision making is not purely rational. Emotional aspects also affect decision making (Andersson & Engelberg, 2006). The taxi-meter effect, for example, increases customer experience and happiness during consumption (Lambrecht & Skiera, 2006). Fun, enjoyment, and happiness are a basic consumption goal sought after when using services (Batra & Ahtola, 1991; O'Curry & Strahilevitz, 2001). Besides achieving the pure utilitarian and functional benefits from consumption, customers often also strive for hedonic, experiential gratification at the same time (K. E. Voss et al., 2003). Thus, the taxi-meter effect increases service consumption benefits and may justify higher costs. Also the insurance effect provides additional benefits; the feeling of being safe from bill shocks which lets customers enjoy consumption more as they do not need to worry about varying or unexpectedly high costs. Similarly, the convenience effect means value for customers. On the one hand, they can save one-time transaction costs in the information and tariff decision phase. Flat-rate tariffs are easy to understand and there is no need for pay-per-use calculations in order to estimate the overall costs. Additionally, there is no need to check monthly bills to see for example if costs are in line with budget which offers a recurring benefit. On the other hand, the convenience effect also continuously lowers transaction costs during consumption for many services. If the payment process is handled manually like for example when paying for every metro ride, a day pass or monthly ticket can significantly lower these costs. Customers for example only need to buy a new ticket every month instead of every day. Hence, depending on the individual subject's appraisal of these psychological benefits, those three flat-rate bias effects may justify higher costs of a flat-rate until certain degrees. But with increasing monetary loss due to flat-rate bias, those benefits plus the one-time switching costs (Burnham, Frels, & Mahajan, 2003) will diminish:

H_{8b}: The higher the monetary loss for customers due to flat-rate bias, the higher the switching probability.

4.1.3 Impact of Flat-Rate Bias on Churn

Following attribution theory, individuals tend to attribute positive, successful outcomes to themselves personally while they rather attribute negative outcomes to external / situational factors (Peterson et al., 1982). Such a behavior is often referred to in literature as self-serving bias, attributional egotism, or egocentric perception (Riess et al., 1981). Causes for this phenomenon come from the "motivation to protect and enhance self-esteem" (i.e. private image) and/or self-presentational concerns (i.e. public image) (Riess et al., 1981, p. 224). For these reasons, individuals want to benefit from positive outcomes while they want to detain negative outcomes from their public and private image.

Applying attribution theory to the situation of a customer who realizes that he or she is paying too much with his or her flat-rate might trigger external attribution: The customer attributes the wrong tariff choice to the service provider assuming deceptive pricing or bad consultation which finally leads to negative feelings towards the service provider (Wong, 2010b). As a result, the customer might not only consider switching the tariff, but also churning away from the current service provider as pricing is the key reason for a customer to churn to competitors (Joo et al., 2002). Accordingly, it is suspected that the psychological value of the convenience, the taxi-meter, and the insurance effects absorb part of this effect if the monetary loss is rather low.

H_{9a}: Customers with flat-rate bias have higher churn rates than customers without flat-rate bias.

H_{9b}: The higher the monetary loss for customers due to flat-rate bias, the higher the churn probability.

4.1.4 Impact of Competitive Position on Flat-Rate Bias Consequences

The central question for service providers now becomes to determine if flat-rate bias customers only switch the tariff like the results of Lambrecht and Skiera (2006) indicate, or if they finally churn like general pricing research predicts. This is likely driven by the competitive position of the service provider. Michael Porter (1980) differentiates between two oppositional generic business-level strategies: differentiation and cost leadership. A differentiation strategy aims at offering services with unique qualities such as high speed, reliability, or customer experience. As premium service providers promote their unique quality and outstanding service level they can be regarded as followers of a differentiation strategy (Choi, Lee, & Chung, 2001). Such a strategy allows the provider to charger higher prices than the industry average (Dess & Davis, 1984) which attracts customers with low price sensitivity (C. W. L. Hill, 1988; Murray, 1988). A cost leadership strategy instead aims at offering services at the lowest price in the market or at least the lowest price to value ratio (Porter, 1980). Low-cost service providers are implementers of a cost leadership strategy (Choi et al., 2001) and attract customers that are very price aware and price sensitive (C. W. L. Hill, 1988; Murray, 1988).

Price sensitivity is an important driver of consumer behavior in terms of price search: "Higher price sensitivity implies that consumers attach greater importance to discovering lower prices and hence will exhibit higher search propensity" (Mehta, Rajiv, & Srinivasan, 2003, p. 69). Additionally to the higher price search propensity, customers with high price sensitivity are also less loyal (Santonen, 2007). Thus price sensitive customers more likely discover the existence of flat-rate bias and, once discovered that they pay too much, are less loyal and more likely to react (switching and/or churn) upon its discovery. In contrast, premium service provider customers have lower price sensitivity resulting in a lower price search propensity and thus a lower likelihood to discover flat-rate bias. Additionally, the sophisticated relationship marketing of premium service providers lowers the price sensitivity of their customers and increases loyalty (Grönroos, 1994). Therefore it is expected:

H_{10}: Low-cost service provider customers show higher reactivity (churn and/or switching) on flat-rate bias than premium provider customers.

Once flat-rate bias gets discovered and customers are willing to react (churn and/or switching), the question is *how* they eventually react (churn or switching). As the attractiveness of alternative offers on the market determines the strength of a customer relationship it is a key driver of customer loyalty (Morgan & Hunt, 1994). Premium service providers focus on a differentiated offering and quality rather than on price resulting in high price levels (Dess & Davis, 1984). Competitive offers from the industry average or low-cost segment are thus very attractive from a financial point of view as they provide high expected savings to customers increasing the risk of churn. For low-cost provider customers instead, their prices are already very low

(Dess & Davis, 1984) and so is the attractiveness of alternative offers. Hyper-competition puts additional pressure on the low-cost segment. Cost advantages erode faster and faster leading to very small price differences among the competitors within their segment (D'Aveni, 1994). Thus the achievable savings from competitive offers are higher for premium service provider customers than for low-cost service provider customers:

> H_{11}: Premium service provider customers have a higher churn probability than low-cost service provider customers.

4.1.5 Overview of Hypotheses H_8 to H_{11}

Table 41 provides an overview of all hypotheses, and Figure 12 shows the conceptual Research model graphically.

Hypothesis	*Prediction*
H_{8a}	Customers with flat-rate bias have higher switching rates than customers without flat-rate bias.
H_{8b}	The higher the monetary loss for customers due to flat-rate bias, the higher the switching probability.
H_{9a}	Customers with flat-rate bias have higher churn rates than customers without flat-rate bias.
H_{9b}	The higher the monetary loss for customers due to flat-rate bias, the higher the churn probability.
H_{10}	Low-cost service provider customers show higher reactivity (churn and/or switching) on flat-rate bias than premium provider customers.
H_{11}	Premium service provider customers have a higher churn probability than low-cost service provider customers.

Table 41—Overview of Hypotheses H_8 to H_{11}

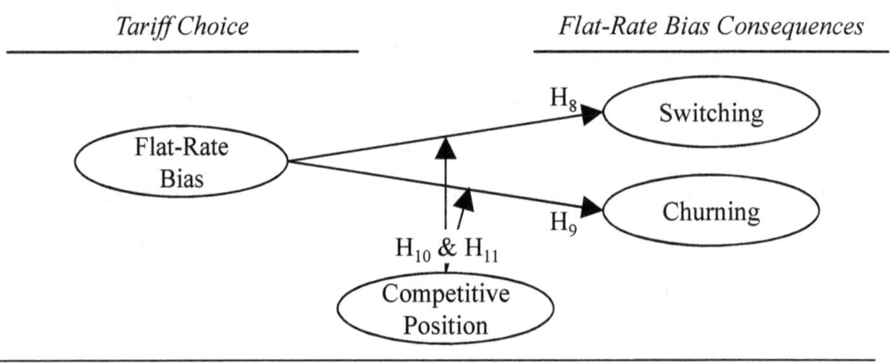

Figure 12—Conceptual Research Model for Hypotheses H_8 to H_{11}

4.2 Empirical Study

4.2.1 Research Approach and Methodology

To test those hypotheses and thus research questions RQ_2 and RQ_3, a combination of transactional data analysis followed by an experimental survey gets applied. At first, Study 7 analyzes research question RQ_2, the consequences of flat-rate bias for Internet Service Provider customers in terms of switching and churn answering hypotheses H_8 and H_9. Study 7 ends with a comparison of the findings with existing research highlighting the differences and providing a potential explanation—the competitive position of the service provider.

Study 8 tackles research question RQ_3 and tests hypotheses H_{10} and H_{11}. The goal is to find out if and how the competitive position of a service provider determines the type of customer reaction upon the discovery of flat-rate bias. Data used to test the hypotheses is a tariff database in combination with a hypothetical scenario survey and a survey on actual mobile telecommunication users analyzing their expected behavior under more realistic conditions.

4.2.2 Study 7: Transactional Data Analysis

4.2.2.1 Research Design

To answer research question RQ_2 (consequences of flat-rate bias on switching and churn) transactional and invoice data from a major German ISP gets analyzed. A cohort based approach tracks 21,490 customers who signed up with the ISP in the first quarter of the observation window over a two years period on a monthly basis. Cohort analysis comes from social science and medical research and observes a group of subjects with common characteristics (in this case the contract start in the first quarter) throughout an observation window (in this case two years) (Menard, 2002). Compared to cross-sectional analyses, cohort analysis is free off any effects due to interpersonal change. For example, cross sectional analysis of ISP customers could lead to wrong conclusions when analyzing effects of customer relationship duration: Long-term customers can show different behavior due to the long relationship with the provider, or because they joined the provider during times where internet usage was totally different from today. Here, cohort analysis excludes potential alternative explanations (Reinartz & Kumar, 2000).

The customers in the sample subscribed to one of four tariffs: (Tariff 1) No fixed monthly fee but a relatively high variable price per minute; (Tariff 2) a medium fixed monthly fee including a specific time allowance plus a lower variable price per minute for any usage in excess; (Tariff 3) a medium fixed monthly fee including a volume allowance plus a medium variable price for any megabyte in excess; and (Tariff 4) a high fixed monthly fee for unlimited usage. Tariff 1 and Tariff 2 use time-based billing whereas Tariff 3 and Tariff 4 are volume-based tariffs; the price differences between the respective small tariffs (Tariff 1 / Tariff 3) and large tariffs (Tariff 2 / Tariff 4) are comparable (€17 vs. €20). Customers can monitor their usage via the ISP's connection manager application and there is no minimum contract duration allowing customers to cancel or switch their contract at any time. Basic descriptive information on the datasets is provided in Table 42.

	Overall	*Tariff 1*	*Tariff 2*	*Tariff 3*	*Tariff 4*
Number of customers [#]	21,490	5,628	3,289	2,077	10,496
Avg. customer age [years]	42.0 (12.6)	43.5 (13.1)	43.7 (12.3)	42.7 (12.6)	40.2 (12.3)
Avg. usage vol. [GB]	6.1 (16.2)	0.1 (0.3)	0.2 (0.7)	0.5 (0.8)	12.3 (20.1)
Avg. usage time [h]	147.2 (222.3)	6.5 (12.6)	18.8 (20.3)	72.0 (136.5)	277.7 (244.4)
Avg. invoice amount [€]	18.4 (14.7)	7.5 (18.5)	17.6 (14.5)	11.7 (18.1)	25.8 (0)
Avg. observed periods [months]	17.9 (6.3)	16.9 (7.2)	17.9 (6.3)	19.4 (5.1)	17.9 (6.3)

Note: Standard deviation in parentheses; allocation of users to tariffs based on tariff in first period.

Table 42—Basic Descriptive Information of Transactional Data

Although Tariff 2 and Tariff 3 are three-part tariffs, they can be treated like flat-rates due to their high allowances in line with other research (Heidenreich & Handrich, 2010; Lambrecht & Skiera, 2006). A user has a flat-rate bias if his chosen tariff with a higher inclusive allowance (in the following FR-tariff) compared to the respective "smaller" tariff (in the following PPU-tariff) results in a higher total invoice. In line with Lambrecht and Skiera (2006) two criterions to define whether a user has a flat-rate bias over his observed lifetime are used: a user experiences "overall" a flat-rate bias if, in sum, the PPU-tariff would have been less expensive; and he "always" exhibits a FRB if the PPU-tariff would have been the cheaper choice for every single month. Hence the criterion "always" is stricter and includes the "overall" criterion.

In the analyses the average amount of the flat-rate bias gets quantified as the average monthly monetary loss incurred to a user due to his bias. To calculate this amount, for every user u with a FR-tariff for each month t the hypothetical invoice amount $inv_{u,t}^{PPU}$ if he had chosen the PPU-tariff gets determined. If a user exhibits a flat-rate bias the resulting average monetary loss is defined as the average difference of the actual and hypothetical invoices $frb_u = avg_t(inv_{u,t}^{PPU} - inv_{u,t}^{FR})$; for users without flat-rate bias this amount is set to zero.

	PPU	*FR*
Number of customers	7,705	13,785
Avg. invoice amount per month	8.6 (δ 18.4)	23.9 (δ 7.9)
Bias criterion "overall"		
Users with FRB	-	41.66 %
Avg. amount of FRB	-	€ 13.51 (δ 5.93)
Bias criterion "always"		
Users with FRB	-	23.97%
Avg. amount of FRB	-	€ 16.26 (δ 2.76)

Table 43—Existence and Amount of Flat-Rate Bias

Regarding the consequences of flat-rate bias, two relationships are investigated in the data. First, the fact that if a user exhibits a flat-rate bias this leads to higher churn or tariff switching probability (H_{8a} and H_{9a}). And second, whether this potential increase depends on the actual amount of the monetary loss incurred due to the flat-rate bias (H_{8b} and H_{9b}).

The first question gets answered by comparing the churn and switching probabilities of users with and without flat-rate bias by calculating the respective proportions $P(churn | FRB)$ and $P(churn | \overline{FRB})$ of users churning within the observation window; and $P(switch | FRB)$ and $P(switch | \overline{FRB})$ for switching. A test for significance of these differences by means of the Mann–Whitney–Wilcoxon test gets conducted to see if the differences are significant.

The latter question is typical for retention studies, which are conducted in many industries such as telecommunications. For this task, both logistic regression and survival analysis are commonly used (Lu, 2002). In this context, survival analysis is preferable since it can handle right-censoring (no information about customer behavior beyond the observation window) more effectively and fully utilizes the duration data (Li, 1995). Especially in this context where there is no minimum contract duration, the customer is continuously evaluating his customership. Logistic regression, however, can only handle dichotomous dependent variables, i.e.: has the customer churned/switched within the observation window or not. Here, survival analysis uses duration data as a continuous parameter and differentiates whether a customer canceled the service in the second or in the 23rd month. In the former case one would assume a much higher propensity to churn. Ignoring this information would reduce the precision of the estimates (Allison, 2010). From the perspective of survival analysis, the question is: how does the monetary loss due to flat-rate bias influence the time until the customer churns or switches the tariff?

As primary specification of the survival model a Weibull hazard function gets applied with shape parameter p and the average amount of monetary loss due to flat-rate bias frb_u of a user u as sole predictor variable: $h(t) = pt^{p-1}e^{\alpha_0+\alpha_1 frb_u}$. This full-parametric survival model is chosen, since it can be more efficient and provide more meaningful results than for instance semi-parametric models (May & Hosmer, 1998). In particular the estimation of the baseline hazard functions allows to making inferences on the actual survival time or churn probabilities, respectively. Robustness of the results was tested with a variety of alternative specifications and models including the popular semi-parametric Cox proportional-hazards model and a basic logistic regression.

The overall adequacy of the model gets confirmed by two common tests: First, a widely popular test based on the plot of the empirically observed Kaplan-Maier cumulative hazards vs. the Cox-Snell residuals (i.e., the cumulative hazard function of the regression model) gets used (David W. Hosmer, Lemeshow, & May, 2008). Second, the Grønnesby and Borgan test gets carried out based on the ranked risk-score with five indicator variables (Grønnesby & Borgan, 1996; S May & Hosmer, 1998).

To evaluate the overall impact of flat-rate bias in terms of company profits, the Customer Lifetime Value gets used. It represents the net present value of all future profits obtained from a customer (Berger & Nasr, 1998). For modeling Customer Lifetime Value, researchers have used different approaches, e.g., with respect to time horizons. The common approach to convert the retention rate into the expected customer lifetime and calculate the present value over this finite period (Gupta & Lehmann, 2003) has been shown to overestimate Customer Lifetime Value (Gupta et al., 2006; Iyengar, Ansari, & Gupta, 2007). Therefore and especially since the observation window is significantly shorter than the expected customer lifetime it is not possible to evaluate the Customer Lifetime Value impact of flat-rate bias based on actual observed changes in customer revenues or profit. Rather one must project the Customer Lifetime Value impact based on the observed changes on an infinite time horizon following Gupta and Lehman (2003):

$$CLV = m\frac{r}{1+i-r}$$

With m = annual gross margin, r = retention rate, i = discount factor. Based on the results of the survival analysis (i.e., the change of expected lifetime with respect to monetary loss due to flat-rate bias) the impact of the monetary loss due to flat-rate bias on the overall Customer Lifetime Value can be estimated: The results of the survival analysis allow to estimate the percent-change c in average lifetime duration d per Euro increase of monetary loss due to flat-rate bias frb:

$$d_{frb} = d \cdot (1+c)^{frb} \quad \text{with} \quad d = \frac{1}{(1-r)}.$$

This allows assessing the effect on the retention rate as

$$r_{frb} = 1 - \frac{1-r}{(1+c)^{frb}}$$

and finally calculating Customer Lifetime Value as a function of flat-rate bias

$$CLV(frb) = (m + frb)\frac{r_{frb}}{1+i-r_{frb}}.$$

The impact of the monetary loss due to flat-rate bias frb can be defined as

$$\frac{CLV(frb) - CLV(0)}{CLV(0)}.$$

4.2.2.2 Empirical Findings

Table 44 shows churn and switching probabilities of users with and without flat-rate bias according to the two criterions. The results indicate that flat-rate bias does not have a significant impact on the switching probability. Hence hypothesis H_{8a} gets rejected. In contrast, users who exhibit flat-rate bias "overall" have a 2.74 percentage points (7.99%) higher churn probability than users without. This difference is even higher for the criterion "always": users that always have a flat-rate bias have 11.22 percentage points (34.34%) higher risk of cancellation. Both differences are significant at $p < .01$ level and thus support H_{9a}.

	Criterion "Overall"			*Criterion "Always"*		
	No FRB	*FRB*	*Delta*	*No FRB*	*FRB*	*Delta*
Switch	17.36 %	16.38 %	-.98pp	16.62 %	17.86 %	1.24pp
Churn	34.28 %	37.02 %	2.74pp**	32.67 %	43.89 %	11.22pp**

** $p < .01$.

Table 44—Differences in Switching and Churn Probabilities

The results of the survival analysis (see Table 45) support the previous analysis. There is no significant impact of the amount of flat-rate bias on the tariff switching probabilities rejecting hypothesis H_{8b}. However for the churn probability the results show that each Euro increase in the monetary loss leads to a significant decrease of customer survival duration by -0.89%. Thus H_{9b} is supported. Figure 13 displays these results in the form of Kaplan-Meier curves of the survival functions, plotted stratified on the bias height.

Variable	*Coeff. α*	*SE*	*95% CI*	*AF*	χ^2	*p*
Model 1 (Churn)						
FRB amount	-.0089	.0021	-.0130 to -.0048	.9911	18.31	<.0001
Scale	.9221	.0140	.8951 to .9499			
Model 2 (Switch)						
FRB amount	.0014	.0023	-.0031 to .0059	1.0014	.38	.5401
Scale	.6138	.0154	.5843 to .6448			

Note: CI = Confidence Interval, AF = Acceleration Factor (e^{α}).

Table 45—Results of Weibull Survival Model

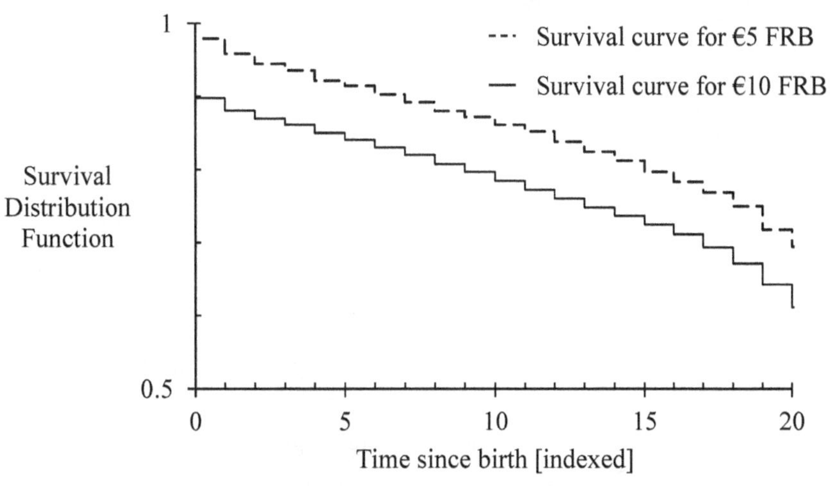

Figure 13—Kaplan-Meier Curves Stratified on Monthly Monetary Loss due to Flat-Rate Bias

For both models the scale parameter is smaller than 1, indicating a general increasing trend in the baseline churn probability over time. This is in line with previous research in the telecommunications industry that found the churn probability to generally increase over time (Li, 1995). In the context of this study, the increase of the churn probability can also be led back to the sustainability of the flat-rate bias effects: As a user gains experience with the flat-rate, the effect of overestimation diminishes, and—following economic theory—his propensity to leave should increase. This rationale should also apply for the insurance effect, as more experience lowers uncertainty. Instead the psychological benefit of the taxi-meter effect (having more fun during usage) and the transactional cost benefit from the convenience effect (less payment effort) should be constant.

Finally a sensitivity analysis by estimating the effect of the flat-rate bias amount with a Cox proportional-hazard model and logistic regression gets conducted (see Table 46 and Table 47). A statistically significant effect of the amount of monetary loss due to the flat-rate bias is only found on the churn probability, with the Cox proportional hazard ratio of 1.015 and the odds ratio of the logistic regression of likewise 1.015. Hence both results indicate that each Euro increase of the amount of monetary loss due to flat-rate bias increases churn probability by 1.5% and are consequently robust with the primary model.

Variable	α	*SE*	*HR*	*HR 95% CI*	χ^2	*p*
Model 1 (Churn)						
FRB amount	.0150	0.0022	1.015	1.011 to 1.019	47.39	<.0001
Model 2 (Switch)						
FRB amount	-.0026	.0036	1.003	.995 to 1.010	.50	.4789

Note: CI = Confidence Interval, HR = Hazard Ratio (e^{α}).

Table 46—Results of Cox Proportional Hazard Survival Model

Variable	α	*SE*	*OR*	*OR 95% CI*	χ^2	*p*
Model 1 (Churn)						
FRB amount	.0149	0.0027	1.015	1.010 to 1.020	29.41	<.0001
Model 2 (Switch)						
FRB amount	-.0020	0.0040	.998	.990 to 1.006	0.25	.6189

Note: CI = Confidence Interval, OR = Odds Ratio (e^{α}).

Table 47—Results of Logistic Regression Model

The results of the survival model show that in the dataset for each one Euro increase of flat-rate bias the average customer lifetime decreases by -0.89% and thus has a negative effect on the Customer Lifetime Value. However on the other hand, since flat-rate bias increases the profit margin, it also has a positive impact on Customer Lifetime Value. Combined, the impact of flat-rate bias on Customer Lifetime Value is in an overall inverse U-shaped relationship with the amount of monetary loss due to flat-rate bias (see Figure 14, assuming 40% gross profit margin and an annual discount rate of 7%). Though this relationship theoretically has a vertex at around €55, Customer Lifetime Value monotonically increases within the practically possible interval, since the maximum amount of flat-rate bias is limited by the price of the flat-rate of around €25 gross. Thus in the data, despite increasing churn rates, flat-rate bias overall has a positive effect on Customer Lifetime Value.

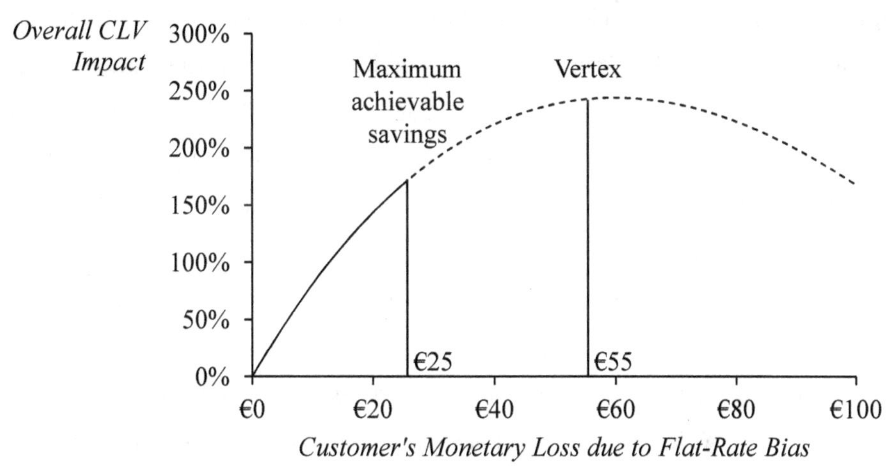

Figure 14—Impact of Monetary Loss due to Flat-Rate Bias on CLV

4.2.2.3 Summary of Study 7

The results are in line with existing research confirming the existence of flat-rate bias (Della Vigna & Malmendier, 2006; Kridel et al., 1993; Mitchell & Vogelsang, 1991; Nunes, 2000). Also in terms of prevalence of flat-rate bias, the results are consistent with those from other studies (e.g., 42% in this study as compared to 38%, 45%, and 76% in other studies, see Table 2, p. 11).

However, the results regarding the consequences of flat-rate bias point into the opposite direction compared to the findings of Lambrecht and Skiera (2006) (see Table 48). Customers with a flat-rate bias in the sample of Lambrecht and Skiera (2006) show a significantly increased switching behavior, whereas customers in this sample have a significantly higher churn rate.

Significant Increase of...		*Lambrecht and Skiera 2006*	*This Study*
...switching	(criterion 1)	*n/s*	*n/s*
...switching	(criterion 2)	~13pp higher switching rate[a]	*n/s*
...churn	(criterion 1)	*n/s*	1.8pp higher churn rate
...churn	(criterion 2)	*n/s*	7.6pp higher churn rate

Note: n/s = no significant difference; a = estimate based on reported percentage point changes for 5 month; figures annualized.

Table 48—Comparison of this Study with Lambrecht and Skiera (2006)

In the study of Lambrecht and Skiera (2006), the degree of customer reactivity (share of customers reacting: switching and/or churn) is higher which could indicate a higher price sensitivity of customers. As Study 7 is based on the data of a premium service provider, this could mean that the data from Lambrecht and Skiera (2006) might be from a low-cost service provider where customers are supposed to have a higher price sensitivity (C. W. L. Hill, 1988; Murray, 1988). This would support hypothesis H_{10} claiming a higher price sensitivity and reactivity of low-cost service provider customers. In the following chapter, this hypothesis gets tested with an experimental survey.

But also the type of reaction differs. The consequence of flat-rate bias is switching in the data of Lambrecht and Skiera (2006), customers in the data from Study 7 directly churn away. Again, this could be explained by the market position of the service provider. As the attractiveness of competitive offers is a main driver for customer loyalty (Morgan & Hunt, 1994) which, following hypothesis H_{11}, is higher for premium service provider customers as in the data of Study 7. Tariff-wise, customers of high price premium providers have many attractive alternatives on the market at a lower price level. This might increase churn probability as customers try to realize the maximum savings possible. For low-cost provider customers instead there is less potential from competitive offers which might make customers stick to their provider and only switch the tariff. Also this hypothesis H_{11} will be tested in Study 8.

4.2.3 Study 8: Experimental Survey with Mobile Telecommunications Customers

4.2.3.1 Research Design

To answer research question RQ_3 ("Does the competitive position of a service provider moderate flat-rate bias consequences?") and hypotheses H_{10} and H_{11}, an experimental survey among mobile telecommunications customers was conducted.

First, a tariff database was compiled in May 2011 containing tariff details of relevant mobile telecommunication flat-rates available in Germany to assess price levels and savings potentials (see Table 49). Additional to common market knowledge relevant service providers and tariffs were identified based on a tariff comparison tool in the Internet (http://www.handyflatrate-preisvergleich.de/). The tariff used for the comparison is an all-net flat-rate including voice minutes to all German fixed and mobile telecommunications networks as this is the most distinct flat-rate tariff. The regular monthly rate for two year contracts excluding effects of temporary promotional offers was used as price for the analysis. Three expert interviews segmented the operators in low-cost and premium providers based on several criteria. These included brand image, advertising expenditure, retail network, technical infrastructure, service quality, and price level (Choi et al., 2001).

Mobile Operator	*Tariff Name*	*Market Segment*	*Monthly Fee [€]*	*Average Fee [€]*
Phonex	All-In-Flat	Low-cost	37.90	Low-cost segment: 38.91
1&1	All-Net-Flat	Low-cost	39.99	
Drillisch Telecom	All-In-Flat	Low-cost	37.90	
Prima	All-Net-Flat	Low-cost	39.85	
Base	Allnet-Flat	Medium	50.00	Medium & Premium segment: 66.84
Flexmobil	Extra	Medium	64.95	
Simfix	Voll-Flat	Medium	59.95	
Congstar	Full-Flat	Medium	59.99	
Vodafone	Superflat-Allnet	Premium	79.95	Premium segment: 83.28
Blackandmine	Allflat	Premium	79.95	
Deutsche Telekom	Complete-Mobile-XL	Premium	89.95	

Table 49—Mobile Telecommunications Flat-Rate Tariff Database

Next, an online survey (see Appendix E) among 211 telecommunications flat-rate customers was conducted using convenience sampling among friends and family. Table 50 shows the socio-demographic information of the respondents:

Criterion	*Value*	*%*
Gender	1: Male	62%
	2: Female	38%
Age	15-25 years	20%
	25-45 years	77%
	45-65 years	3%
Gross Household Income	1: < €1,500 per month	14%
	2: €1,500 - €2,499 per month	9%
	3: €2,500 - €3,499 per month	12%
	4: €3,500 - €4,499 per month	17%
	5: €4,500 - €5,499 per month	11%
	6: €5,500 - €6,499 per month	6%
	7: €6,500 - €7,499 per month	7%
	8: > € 7,500 per month	24%

Table 50—Socio-Demographic Characteristics of Respondents for Study 8

In the introduction pay-per-use, volume packages and flat-rate pricing was defined to ensure that all respondents have the same understanding of the relevant tariffs. Customers with pay-per-use pricing were filtered out while customers with volume packages were treated like flat-rate customers (with respectively adjusted wording throughout the survey) in line with the approach used in Study 7 and Lambrecht and Skiera (2006).

In order to rule out potential problems of endogeneity, respondents were assigned randomly to two groups. Group one had to complete the questionnaire based on their real actual service provider. They were asked to name their current service provider in order to classify them later as premium or low-cost service provider customers. Next they had to state their current voice tariff and also their monthly flat fee. The advantage of this approach is to have real premium and low-cost provider customers but it has the risk of potential endogeneity problems. Group two was assigned to two hypothetical scenarios. Half of them were assigned to being customer of the hypothetical low-cost operator "CheapTel", and the other half to the premium provider "PrimeTel". A short text described the qualities in terms of image, service level and pricing of the respective provider. Specifically, the monthly fee for the flat-rate of CheapTel was given with €40 and €80 for PrimeTel. Those prices were based on typical prices of the low-cost and premium segment of the German market based on the tariff database. This approach relies on the ability of respondents to act as being customer of a hypothetical provider but eliminates potential endogeneity problems.

As it is not possible to measure the awareness of having a flat-rate bias (i.e. the probability of its discovery) in such an artificial experimental condition, both groups were confronted with the following statement: "Scientific research has shown that many flat-rate customers do not leverage their tariff and waste money compared to pay-per-use pricing." In order to measure their (intended) reactivity on flat-rate bias respondents were further told: "Assume you could quit your current flat-rate contract immediately without any switching cost and you could keep your current telephone number. How much savings compared to your current flat-rate tariff would it need to make you switch to pay-per-use or churn to a pay-per-use offer from a competitor?" Price sensitivity was measured twice (once for switching and once for churning) using a scale adopted from Van Westendorp's Price Sensitivity Meter (PSM) (Westendorp, 1976). Respondents were asked to name four price deltas: (PD_1) which price difference is so low you don't even consider switching/churning, (PD_2)

at which price delta you start thinking about switching/churning, (PD_3) which price delta would make sticking to the flat-rate (at your provider) really hard for you, and (PD_4) at which price delta would you definitely switch/churn?

4.2.3.2 Empirical Findings

Independent samples T-tests among the real customers (Group 1, see Table 51) show for premium provider customers a significantly higher monthly bill value than for low-cost provider customers confirming the classification. Price sensitivities for switching are higher in the low-cost segment (lower tolerated absolute price delta) but the differences are not significant which could be due to the relatively small sample size. The absolute tolerated price deltas PD_1 and PD_2 for churn are lower in the low-cost segment as expected but not significant as well. But the critical price deltas for churn PD_3 ("Which price delta would make sticking to the flat-rate at your provider really hard for you?": $M_{low\text{-}cost} = 10.1$, $M_{premium} = 13.3$, $T(55) = 2.0$, $p < .05$) and PD_4 ("At which price delta would you definitely churn?": $M_{low\text{-}cost} = 15.6$, $M_{premium} = 20.8$, $T(94) = 2.7$, $p < .05$) are significantly higher in the low-cost than in the premium segment. Thus the expected reactivity on flat-rate bias (switching and/or churn) is higher for low-cost service provider customers confirming hypothesis H_{10}. Socio-demographic information does not differ significantly between the two segments and can be ruled out as potential alternative explanation.

	Premium (n=34)		*Low-Cost (n=62)*			
	M	*SE*	*M*	*SE*	*df*	*T*
Churn PD_1	8.2	1.1	6.6	0.5	49	1.3
Churn PD_2	13.5	1.5	10.6	0.7	50	1.8
Churn PD_3	13.3	1.4	10.1	0.8	55	2.0*
Churn PD_4	20.8	2.0	15.6	1.0	94	2.7*
Switching PD_1	6.2	.9	5.5	.5	94	.7
Switching PD_2	11.1	1.3	9.1	.7	94	1.4
Switching PD_3	10.6	1.1	9.0	.8	94	1.1
Switching PD_4	17.0	1.8	13.6	1.0	94	1.8
Gender	1.4	.1	1.4	.1	94	.2
Age	28.7	1.1	30.3	.9	94	-1.1
Income	5.2	.4	4.5	.3	94	1.1
Bill-value	56	7.4	35	2.5	43	2.7**

*$p < .05$, **$p < .01$.

Notes: Levene's test for equality of variances was taken into account.

Table 51—Independent Samples T-Test of Price Sensitivities for Real Customers

Independent samples T-tests (see Table 52) for the hypothetical scenarios support these results and thus hypothesis H_{10}.

	Premium (n=46)		*Low-Cost (n=49)*			
	M	*SE*	*M*	*SE*	*df*	*T*
Churn PD_1	7.0	0.8	6.3	0.6	93	0.7
Churn PD_2	11.1	1.2	9.7	1.0	93	0.9
Churn PD_3	12.0	1.3	8.8	0.8	93	2.2*
Churn PD_4	18.1	1.8	13.8	1.3	93	2.0*
Switching PD_1	5.5	.6	6.2	.7	93	-.8
Switching PD_2	9.7	1.0	9.5	1.0	93	.2
Switching PD_3	9.9	1.1	8.4	.8	93	1.1
Switching PD_4	16.3	1.7	13.1	1.3	93	1.5
Gender	1.3	.1	1.5	.1	93	-1.9
Age	29.8	.9	30.5	1.0	93	-.5
Income	4.6	.4	4.6	.3	93	.1
Bill-value	36	6.0	45	16.5	93	-.5

$*p < .05$.

Notes: Levene's test for equality of variances was taken into account.

Table 52—Independent Samples T-Test of Price Sensitivities for Hypothetical Scenarios

To predict the type of reaction (churn versus switching) for the two segments (premium versus low-cost), the given external market conditions must be taken into account as they determine the scope of action for customers. To prepare price sensitivity curves, the average of PD_3 and PD_4 are used as approximation for the churn-critical price delta, since the actual value should lie between "would barely not churn" (PD_3) and "definitely churn" (PD_4). Figure 15 and Figure 16 reflect the higher price sensitivity of low-cost customers with a steeper slope of the respective curve: The expected churn probability for a given monthly saving is higher in the case of low-cost service provider customers compared to premium provider customers.

In order to contrast the price sensitivity and the attractiveness of alternatives in the market, the potential savings per segment are mapped to the respective price sensitivity curve (see Figure 15 and Figure 16). The potential saving for the low-cost segment was determined based on the delta of the average monthly fee of €38.91 and the cheapest low-cost provider tariff of €37.90 (see Table 49) resulting in around one Euro. In the premium segment the delta between the average monthly premium provider fee of €83.28 and the average monthly fee of the premium and medium segment operators of €66.84 (see Table 49) was used as it would not be expected that a premium provider customer switches to a no frills low-cost carrier directly. Hence the expected savings in the premium segment are at least €16.

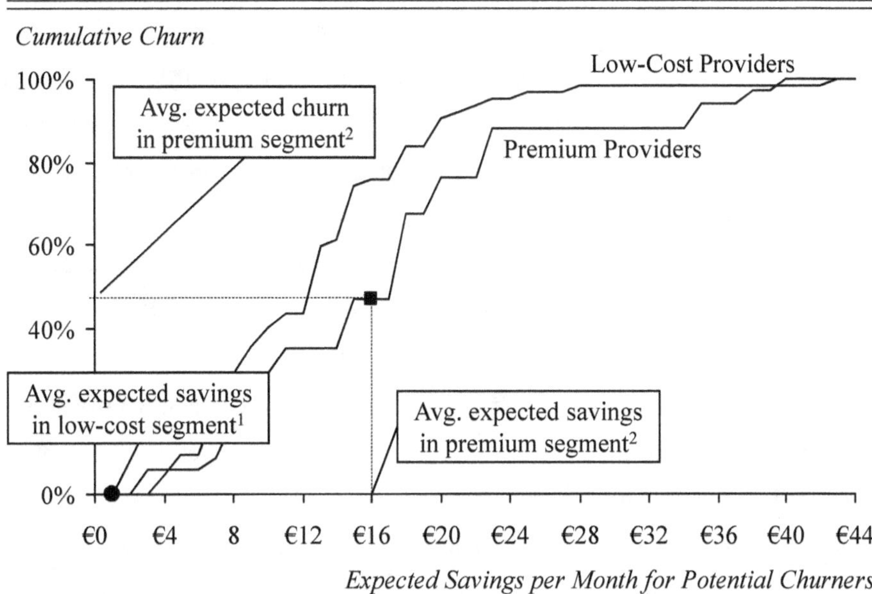

Notes: [1] Avg. monthly fee of low-cost service provider minus min. monthly fee of low-cost service provider; [2] Avg. monthly fee of premium service provider minus avg. monthly fee of all service provider besides low-cost service providers.

Figure 15—Price Sensitivity Curves and Savings Potential for Real Customers

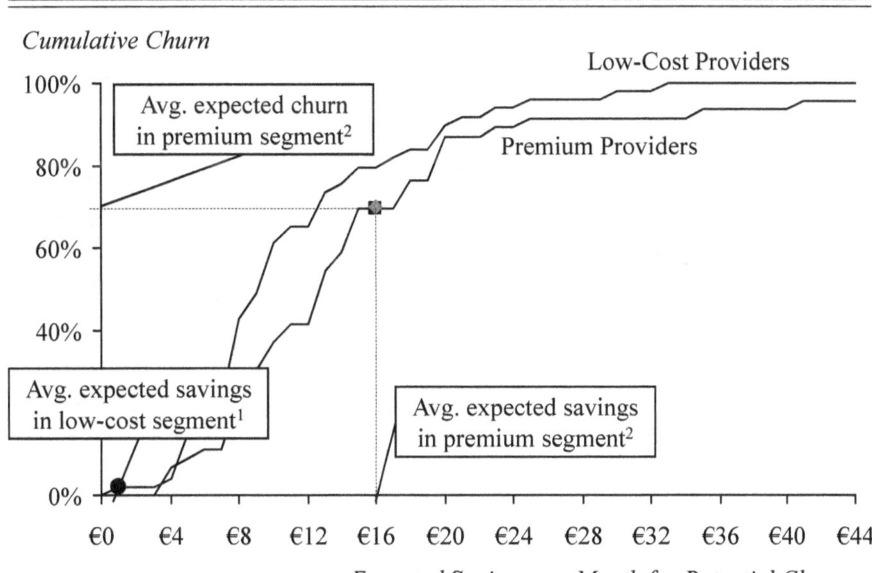

Notes: [1] Avg. monthly fee of low-cost service provider minus min. monthly fee of low-cost service provider; [2] Avg. monthly fee of premium service provider minus avg. monthly fee of all service provider besides low-cost service providers.

Figure 16—Price Sensitivity Curves and Savings Potential for Hypothetical Customers

Taking the actually achievable potential savings per segment (low-cost: €1, premium: €16) on the x-axis reveals the expected churn rates on the y-axis. Despite the higher price sensitivity, the achievable savings in the low-cost segment of one Euro would lead to an expected cumulative churn of 0% in Group 1 (real customers) and 2% in Group 2 (hypothetical scenarios). In contrast, the cumulative churn of premium customers given achievable savings by the market of €16 would be 47%[4] in Group 1 (real customers) and 70%[4] in Group 2 (hypothetical scenarios).

Thus, despite the higher price sensitivity of low-cost customers, the financially most viable option in the absence of attractive competitive offers is to optimize their tariff within the provider, i.e., switch to pay-per-use. In contrast, customers in the premium segment will find significant savings potential and thus are likely to not only switch their tariff but also to change their provider. Thus, the competitive position of a service provider determines the consequences of flat-rate bias. Premium provider customers show a higher risk of churn confirming hypothesis H_{11}.

4.2.3.3 Summary of Study 8

Study 8 shows that the market position of a service provider determines the consequences of flat-rate bias. Customers experiencing monetary loss due to flat-rate bias have three choices to react. First they can just stick to the flat-rate if the value of the flat-rate bias effects justifies the monetary loss for them. If the monetary loss exceeds the perceived value from the flat-rate bias effects, they can either switch their tariff within the current provider, or churn to a competitor. This type of reaction depends on the market position of the service provider as shown in the experimental survey. Premium and low-cost mobile telecommunications customers reported their intended reactions upon the discovery of flat-rate bias for their current telecommunications provider (Group 1) as well as for a hypothetical scenario (Group

[4] These churn rates cannot be compared with real churn rates due to several reasons. Most of all, an experimental survey is an artificial situation. Customers were told about flat-rate bias and thus were sensitive towards the topic and had 100% flat-rate bias awareness. In real life it is unlikely that all customers are aware of having a flat-rate bias—only a fraction will know about their flat-rate usage level at all. Furthermore, respondents were told that there are no switching costs, which is also unrealistic leading to higher churn rates.

2). The results in both groups are identical and show higher reactivity upon the discovery of flat-rate bias in the low-cost segment with a higher risk of churn in the premium segment. This leads to the following anticipated customer behavior: Low-cost service provider customers show a higher reactivity on the monetary loss form flat-rate bias. But due to the limited attractiveness of alternative offers, the only way to financially optimize their tariff choice is switching to pay-per-use. Premium service provider customers instead show a lower reactivity on the monetary loss from flat-rate bias. But due to the highly financially attractive competitive offers (Morgan & Hunt, 1994), their reaction is rather churning to a competitor.

4.3 Discussion

4.3.1 Summary of Studies 7 and 8

Studies 7 and 8 investigate the consequences of flat-rate bias—specifically switching and churn probabilities and eventually the impact on the customer lifetime value. The analysis of transactional data together with an experimental survey answers the posed research questions and hypotheses adequately (see Table 53).

Hypothesis		*Study 7*	*Study 8*
RQ_2:	*Does flat-rate bias increase tariff switching and customer churn?*		
H_{8a}:	Customers with flat-rate bias have higher switching rates than customers without flat-rate bias.	✗	-
H_{8b}:	The higher the monetary loss for customers due to flat-rate bias, the higher the switching probability.	✗	-
H_{9a}:	Customers with flat-rate bias have higher churn rates than customers without flat-rate bias.	✓	-
H_{9b}:	The higher the monetary loss for customers due to flat-rate bias, the higher the churn probability.	✓	-
RQ_3:	*Does the competitive position of a service provider moderate flat-rate bias consequences?*		
H_{10}:	Low-cost service provider customers show higher reactivity (churn and/or switching) on flat-rate bias than premium provider customers.	-	✓
H_{11}:	Premium service provider customers have a higher churn probability than low-cost service provider customers.	-	✓

Notes: – = not applicable, ✓ = hypothesis confirmed, ✗ = hypothesis not confirmed.

Table 53—Overview of Hypotheses H_8 to H_{11} Test Results

4.3.2 Theoretical Implications

The findings of Study 7 and 8 contribute to flat-rate bias theory at least fourfold. First, Study 7 confirms with transactional data of 21,490 customers the existence of flat-rate bias for Internet access and hence adds to the body on this subject matter. Though flat-rate bias has been observed already in a number of cases (see Table 2), these findings underline the pervasiveness and relevance of this phenomenon.

Second, Study 7 shows that customers who exhibit flat-rate bias have significantly higher churn probabilities. Whereas this is contrary to the current notion of flat-rate bias research predicting no negative impact on customer churn (Lambrecht & Skiera, 2006), it is in line with general research on customer loyalty and tariff choice predicting customers to be more loyal if they are on the correct rate plan (Iyengar et al., 2007; Wong, 2010b). This supports attribution theory (Peterson et al., 1982) predicting that customers attribute the failure of the wrong tariff choice to the provider and as a consequence lose loyalty and churn. In addition, the findings reconfirm the relevance of standard economic theory (Brown & Sibley, 1986) for customer loyalty in the context of flat-rate bias. Whereas behavioral decision research (Andersson & Engelberg, 2006) emphasizes the relevance of socio-psychological effects to explain why customers choose flat-rates although pay-per-use would be more economical for them, the results show that in the long-term economic theory has high validity. Customers eventually seem to regret their psychologically driven decision and churn to an economically more attractive tariff.

Third, Study 8 comparing the reactivity of premium versus low-cost provider customers on flat-rate bias provides a potential explanation for these controversial findings. Table 48 shows that customers in the data of Lambrecht and Skiera (2006) show a higher reactivity (switching and/or churn) of 13 percentage points as compared to 7.6 percentage points in the transactional data of Study 7. A reason could be that the data from Lambrecht and Skiera (2006) might be from a low-cost provider as the results in this dissertation indicate that low-cost provider customers show a higher price sensitivity (C. W. L. Hill, 1988; Murray, 1988) and that more price sensitive customers are more likely to engage in price search (Mehta et al., 2003). The oppositional consequences could as well be explained by the competitive position (Porter, 1980). Flat-rate bias in the data of this dissertation leads to churn, anticipated by the fact that the data come from a premium service provider allowing for high savings from competitive offers. This confirms social exchange theory's notion that the attractiveness of competitive offers determines the strength of the customer-firm relationship or loyalty (Morgan & Hunt, 1994). In contrast, the consequence of flat-rate bias in the case of Lambrecht and Skiera (2006) is switching as the attractiveness of competitive offers in the low-cost segment is very limited. Furthermore it seems like attribution theory is not as decisive in the low-cost segment as it is in the premium segment. A reason could be the different customer-company relationships. Premium providers support their customers with individual and personal consultation when choosing an appropriate tariff. Customers then attribute the wrong tariff choice to bad consultation. In the low-cost market, customers rather use self-service over the internet choosing the tariff by themselves. This makes external attributions harder. Thus economic theory becomes the decisive element, and due to the lack of alternatives from competitors, low-cost provider customers just switch to the pay-per-use tariff within their current provider avoiding the transaction costs of churning to another competitor (Burnham et al., 2003).

Fourth, the transactional data show that the increase in churn depends on the amount of monetary loss due to flat-rate bias. Small amounts of monetary loss only lead to a slight increase in churn. A reason might be that the psychological value of the flat-rate bias effects—specifically the convenience, the insurance, and the taxi-meter effects—lower the negative impact. Customers see an additional value of having no need for pay-per-use calculations, more comfortable payment mechanisms, not having to think about the cost while using a service, and being safe from unexpectedly high bill amounts. Increasing monetary loss exceeds these benefits and overestimation might become visible to customers offering no additional value. This finding implies that behavioral decision theory can outweigh standard economic theory until a certain degree of economic loss. Low amounts of monetary loss are bearable for customers following behavioral economics but the higher the monetary losses the less behavioral economics and the more standard economic theory explains customer behavior.

4.3.3 Managerial Implications

Managers find themselves in a double bind. On the one hand, flat-rate bias is a significant source of profit since even a small flat-rate bias of €2 to €3 could increase customer profits by 20% to 50%. In the telecommunications industry, for example, up to half of the revenue is contributed by financially non-optimal rate plans (Wong, 2010b). On the other hand, management guides preach "zero defections", the focus on customer loyalty. Reichheld and Sasser's (1990) illustration of how ever increasing profits over time add up to a multiple of the initial base profits is ubiquitous. In this situation, the results from Study 7 and 8 can help managers to decide how to handle customers with flat-rate bias, and to determine the right trade-off between revenue increase and lifetime maximization by taking the competitive position of the service provider into account.

In the low-cost segment, there do not seem to arise any negative consequences of capitalizing on the customers' flat-rate bias for customer loyalty. If the value from the flat-rate bias effects does not justify the monetary loss incurred from their non-optimal tariff choice, customers still tend to stay with the service provider due to a lack of attractive alternatives. Rather than to churn, the results suggest that they optimize their spending by choosing a more economical tariff within the same operator. Hence for managers in this segment, flat-rate bias is a desirable effect that they can try to foster, e.g., by triggering the causes of flat-rate bias with their marketing activities (Lambrecht & Skiera, 2006) or by "hedonizing" their service experience as shown in chapter 3.3.3.

In contrast, in the premium segment flat-rate bias has a negative impact on customer loyalty. In order to determine whether to proactively mitigate these tendencies, managers should assess the consequences both from a financial and a reputational perspective. First, since these consequences of flat-rate bias, i.e., increasing profits and decreasing customer lifetime, take a converse effect, managers need to assess the overall Customer Lifetime Value impact. The overall Customer Lifetime Value effect depends on the extent to which monetary loss due to flat-rate bias increases the customers' propensity to churn versus the respective profit gains of customers paying too much. In particular, the monetary loss due to flat-rate bias seems to be in an inverse U-shaped relationship with the Customer Lifetime Value. Low amounts of monetary loss lead to only slightly increased churn that is compensated by the additional revenues. After a certain amount of monetary loss due to flat-rate bias this relationship changes. From that point on (vertex of the inverse U-shaped curve), the increased churn devours the additional revenues and leads to a negative impact of flat-rate bias on the Customer Lifetime Value. In the context of the ISP in Study 7, a positive effect can be observed overall. In other contexts, this effect can easily become negative, and doing nothing can be dangerous. Drivers determining the overall Customer Lifetime Value impact are the population specific effect size of monetary loss due to flat-rate bias on customer retention (e.g., -.89% customer lifetime for every Euro monetary loss), and the average customer profits (i.e., monthly contribution of every customer to the company's profit).

Figure 17 shows a sensitivity analysis for the impact of the monetary loss due to flat-rate bias on the overall Customer Lifetime Value depending on various effect strengths. If the impact of flat-rate bias on the retention rate would be -5% instead of -.89%, the overall Customer Lifetime Value would already be negative for all customers experiencing monetary loss due to flat-rate bias of more than €10 per month. This makes sense because the stronger the negative impact of flat-rate bias on customer retention (i.e., the more customers churn for every Euro of monetary loss), the less the increased profits due to flat-rate bias can compensate for the reduced customer base.

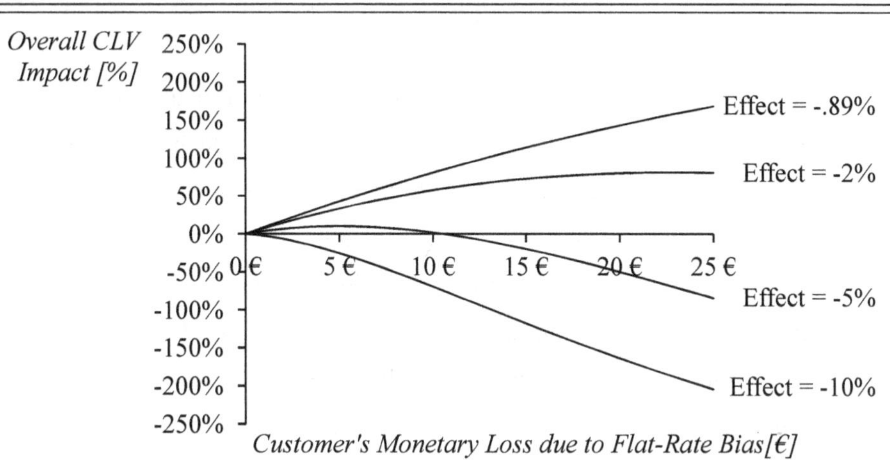

Figure 17—Impact of Monetary Loss due to Flat-Rate Bias on CLV depending on Effect Size

Figure 18 shows a sensitivity analysis for the impact of the monetary loss due to flat-rate bias on the overall Customer Lifetime Value depending on various customer profit margins. For the case that one customer only contributes with €5 to the company, the loss of such a customer is lower than the additional profit from paying too much under the flat-rate tariff. If one customer is more valuable and for example contributes with €20 per month to the provider's profits, the loss of such a valuable customer is much more severe than the additional profit from paying from flat-rate bias.

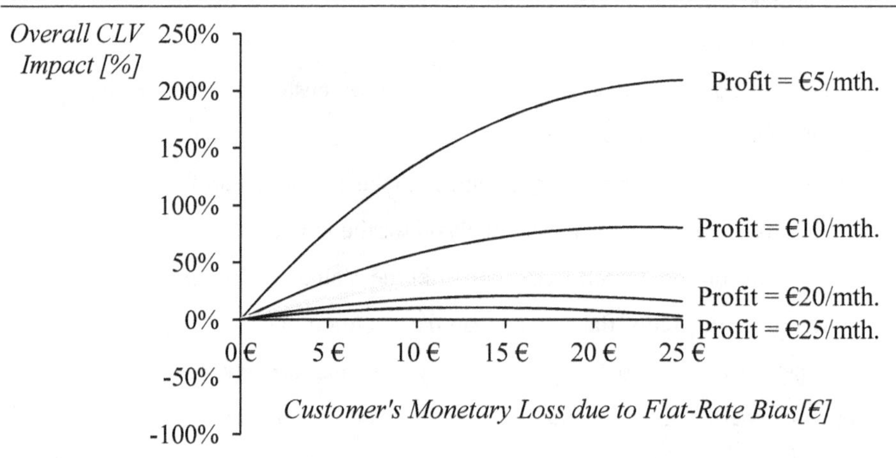

Figure 18—Impact of Monetary Loss due to Flat-Rate Bias on CLV depending on Customer Profit

Thus, mangers must measure these key variables (customer profitability, effect of flat-rate bias on retention) to determine the consequences of flat-rate bias for their company.

However, managers should consider negative word-of-mouth as a result of flat-rate bias. Customers that experience a monetary loss due to their flat-rate bias are likely to attribute the wrong tariff choice to the service provider causing negative sentiments and discontent with their relationship to the firm (Peterson et al., 1982; Riess et al., 1981). As a result of their dissatisfaction they are likely to express their disappointment in the form of negative word-of-mouth (Wangenheim, 2005). This effect, too, is likely to be particularly high for high levels of flat-rate bias.

Hence, for direct financial as well as for reputational reasons, managers in premium contexts should consider managing customers with very high levels of flat-rate bias proactively. One possibility is to approach customers at risk and offer them to switch to a pay-per-use tariff. Alternatively, and in order to reduce flat-rate bias without affecting customer revenues, they might also try to increase customers' usage levels; in the ISP context for example by highlighting or offering new content such as IPTV channels or complimentary video-on-demand vouchers.

4.3.4 Limitations and Further Research

Studies 7 and 8 have several limitations that need to be mentioned and that suggest topics for further research. First, the analyses are all in the domain of telecommunications. Similar investigations in other industries could increase external validity of the findings. However, the telecommunications industry was among the origins of all flat-rate bias research and the results have so far matched all other investigated sectors as well.

Second, only parameters directly related to flat-rate bias are included in the survival analysis due to data availability. An omitted variable bias cannot completely be excluded. There may be more factors determining the reaction to flat-rate bias, such as household income, product involvement, etc. Future research will have to replicate Study 7 in other contexts and extend it by investigating the effect of other parameters to confirm the results. Similarly, when investigating the service providers' competitive position as moderating factor for the consequences of flat-rate bias no other potential moderators influencing the consequences of flat-rate bias have been taken into account. Also the survey is comparably small in size and due to privacy regulations it was not possible to match the survey with the transactional data.

Third, besides an increase of churn probability due to flat-rate bias, also an increase in the baseline churn probability over time is observed. This could be attributed to a wear off of the overestimation effect as the user gains experience, but this cannot be substantiated empirically. Research investigating the sustainability of the flat-rate bias effects would provide a valuable contribution in this domain.

Finally, in an effort to provide further guidance for managers, future research should focus on mitigation strategies for increased churn rates due to flat-rate bias. In many industries, especially in the mobile telecommunications industry, several companies introduce pricing schemes that prevent or at least attenuate flat-rate bias, such as "flex" rate plans which give subscribers the best service rate based on their actual usage (Wong, 2010b). These could serve as basis for scholars to derive best practices.

5 Conclusion

5.1 Summary

This dissertation extends flat-rate bias research in two dimensions—drivers of flat-rate bias effects and thus flat-rate bias variance (research gap 1), and a more differentiated understanding of the consequences in terms of loyalty by identifying a potential moderator (research gap 2).

To fill research gap 1, five tariff choice experiments (Studies 1-5) tested the impact of hedonic and utilitarian consumption goals on flat-rate bias effects and subsequently flat-rate bias using various approaches to generate consumption goal variance. As a result, hedonic consumption goals have been found to drive flat-rate bias effects as mediators that subsequently increase flat-rate bias answering research question RQ_1 ("Do service consumption goals affect flat-rate bias effects and subsequently flat-rate bias?").

Filling the second research gap, a combination of transactional data analysis (Study 7) together with an experimental survey (Study 8) re-investigated the consequences of flat-rate bias on customer loyalty—namely switching and churning. The cohort based analysis of 21,490 ISP customers (Study 7) reveals that not all flat-rate bias customers are being happy about paying too much as Lambrecht and Skiera found in their data (2006). Flat-rate bias customers show a significantly increased risk of churn while switching gets not affected answering research question RQ_2 ("Does flat-rate bias increase tariff switching and customer churn?"). The experimental survey (Study 8) shows that the consequences of flat-rate bias depend on the competitive position of the service provider answering research questions RQ_3 ("Does the competitive position of a service provider moderate flat-rate bias consequences?"). While low-cost service provider flat-rate bias customers mainly react with higher switching, premium service provider flat-rate bias customers have a higher risk of churn.

Detailed discussions on the theoretical and managerial implications as well as limitations can be found in the chapters 3.3 and 4.3 respectively. The overall theoretical and managerial implications are shown in the following chapters 5.2 and 5.3 before stating areas for further research in chapter 5.4.

5.2 Theoretical Implications

The main contribution of this dissertation is the extension of current flat-rate bias research by service specific factors. The pioneers of flat-rate bias research discovered its existence (e.g., Train et al., 1987), and in a second phase, studies identified and clustered its causes, and investigated its consequences (e.g., Lambrecht & Skiera, 2006). This dissertation confirms various theories of the first two phases, like for instance, prospect theory, mental accounting, option value, wishful thinking, guilt and justification, transaction cost theory, or risk aversion; it highlights the need to extend the convenience effect to cover the payment process while service usage besides only the initial decision; and it shows that both, standard economic and behavioral decision theory are relevant for explaining customer behavior—depending on the amount of monetary loss due to flat-rate bias. The detailed findings can be found in chapters 3.3.2 and 4.3.2.

Overall, this dissertation starts a third phase of flat-rate bias research investigating factors beyond current flat-rate bias research. Specifically it identifies a driver of flat-rate bias (the consumption goal) that is fully mediated by the flat-rate bias effects and a moderator of its consequences (the competitive position of the service provider). This extends flat-rate bias research as shown in Figure 19.

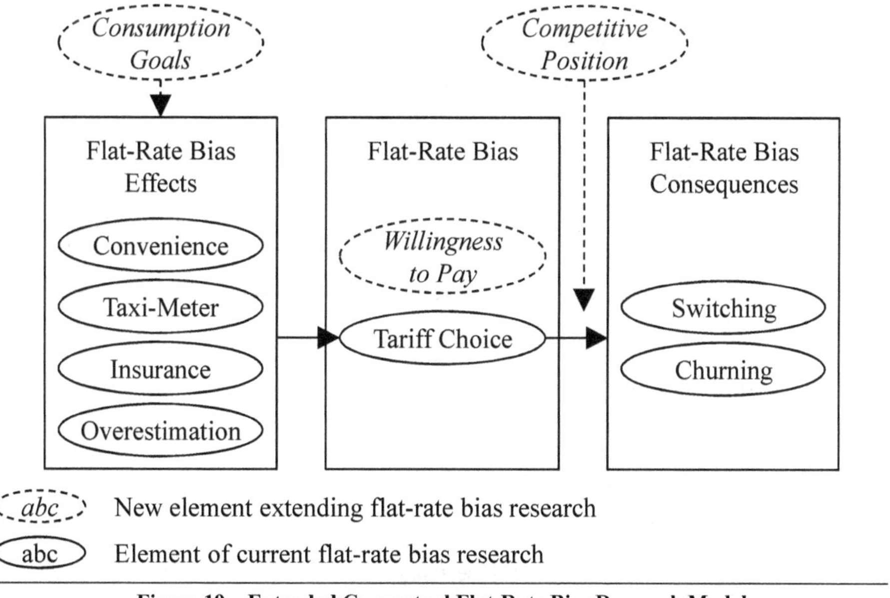

Figure 19—Extended Conceptual Flat-Rate Bias Research Model

Current flat-rate bias research looks at causes of flat-rate bias only from a behavioral economics point of view reflecting consumer psychology. Flat-rate bias gets explained solely by consumer characteristics and does not incorporate service specific factors. The four flat-rate bias effects describe consumers' preferences towards the flat-rate tariff out of personal convenience, for the sake of "cost-free" enjoyment, to insure against unexpected losses, and out of usage overestimation. This dissertation extends flat-rate bias research by service (provider) specific factors.

The consumption goals influence flat-rate bias causes and subsequently flat-rate bias and strongly depend on the service. Some services for example are pure utilitarian means to an end (e.g., using public transportation to get from A to B), others are purely hedonic (e.g., riding the rollercoaster in an amusement park). As Study 1 shows, the same subjects show different levels of flat-rate bias for those two different services depending on the consumption goals.

Also the consequences of flat-rate bias vary depending on service provider characteristics. While customers of low-cost providers only show increased switching behavior, premium provider customers have a higher risk of churn.

These observations cannot be explained or predicted by the current model of flat-rate bias research. Therefore this dissertation extends the conceptual model of flat-rate bias research by the service specific driver of consumption goals influencing flat-rate bias effects, and the service provider dependent moderator of the competitive position determining the consequences of flat-rate bias.

5.3 Managerial Implications

In addition to the detailed managerial implications in chapter 3.3.3 and 4.3.3, this chapter jointly summarizes the key implications for practitioners. Service pricing managers might wonder if they should introduce a flat-rate tariff or not, or if there is need for action regarding their existing flat-rate bias customers. Understanding the consumption goals of their services and their competitive position within the relevant market helps them with such tasks. Flat-rates can be a sustainable win-win situation for providers and customers especially if the service fulfills hedonic consumption goals. Customers then can enjoy service usage without thinking about the cost and are safe from bill shocks, while providers can benefit from constant revenues at a higher level than with pay-per-use. Fostering and promoting the hedonic service experience can further increase these benefits for the providers (see 3.3.3 for details).

However, depending on the competitive position within the market, providers must be careful. In the premium segment, they should regularly analyze the switching and churn behavior of their flat-rate bias customers. Depending on the amount of monetary loss there might be a negative overall impact of flat-rate bias on the Customer Lifetime Value when the negative impact of churn in the long-term is higher than the interim short-term benefits of higher flat-rate bias revenues (see 4.3.3 for details). In such a situation, service providers are advised to approach those endangered customers offering the opportunity to switch their tariff and preventing them to churn away. In the low-cost segment, this is less of a problem as potential savings from competitive offers are expectedly low and so customers mainly optimize their tariff by switching without churn.

5.4 Limitations and Further Research

Detailed limitations of this dissertation are discussed in chapters 3.3.4 and 4.3.4 based on the chosen approaches and used methodologies. Overall, this thesis investigated only two factors determining the existence and consequences of flat-rate bias. However, there are likely to be other factors that might influence flat-rate bias effects, tariff choice and flat-rate bias consequences. Figure 20 makes an attempt to cluster those potential factors into four groups: further *flat-rate bias effects* complementing the four existing effects, *moderators* determining the impact of flat-rate bias effects on tariff choice and subsequently its consequences, additional *drivers* of flat-rate bias effects, flat-rate bias, or its consequences, and potential *negative side effects* of flat-rate bias on tariff choice and customer tariff loyalty.

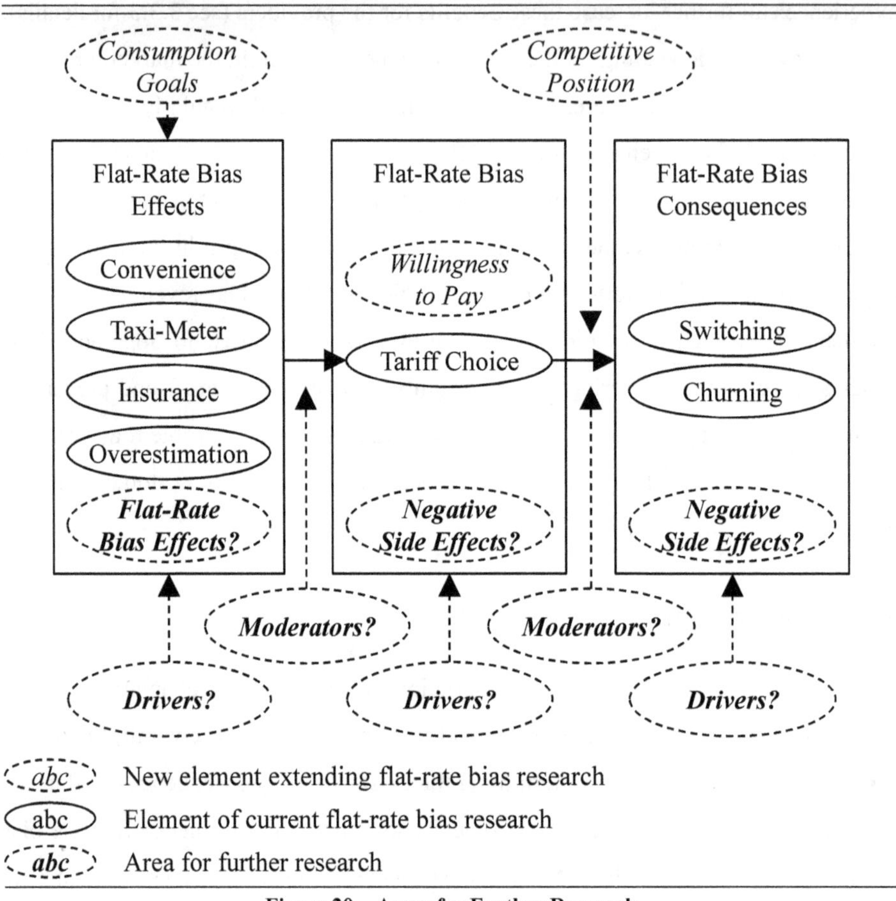

Figure 20—Areas for Further Research

Future research should check if there are other consumer related flat-rate bias effects (e.g., a "flexibility effect" against the commitment to a flat-rate) and investigate further potential service specific drivers and moderators of flat-rate bias. The six service characteristics used in chapter 3.2.3 to maintain ceteris paribus conditions for the tariff choice experiments can be used as starting point:

- How does (1) the contractual setting influence the four flat-rate bias effects? For example following the discussion of 3.3.2 on the significance of the convenience effect, it is expected that the convenience effect has only limited impact in subscription models whereas it might become a strong flat-rate bias driver in situations without a contractual boundary where payments have to be done manually following transaction cost theory (Nunes, 2000).

- Has (2) the integrated factor an impact on flat-rate bias? The taxi-meter effect, for example, might become stronger if the consumer is central element of the service delivery like in a taxi-ride as compared to car checkups where he only submits his belonging. A decisive element could be the intensity of the service experience (personal versus indirectly via belongings) that might determine the perceived pain of paying (Lambrecht & Skiera, 2006).
- Does (3) the time frame change flat-rate bias effects? It could be argued that for a long-term commitment to a health club (e.g., two year contract) wishful thinking (Einhorn & Hogarth, 1986) and thus the overestimation effect is stronger compared to a short term 3-months period which can be better planned in advance.
- Also (4) the price level could drive flat-rate bias effects. Especially the need for insurance should depend on the amount of money involved triggering risk and loss aversion (Kahneman & Tversky, 1979; Nunes, 2000).
- Do (5) the frequency of use and (6) the variability of usage determine flat-rate bias effects? Overestimation should be more likely to occur if the expected usage variability is high and the frequency low. But also the insurance effect is likely to rely on these two factors.

Understanding all factors that influence flat-rate bias is very important as managers of service providers need to understand the circumstances under which flat-rate bias is beneficial or cumbersome to best design their offerings and treat their flat-rate bias customer base. They can increase flat-rate bias and thus profits through "hedonizing" their services but they need to know when negative consequences outweigh the benefits. Therefore it is important to check that there are no unwanted side effects of flat-rate bias like negative word-of-mouth (Wangenheim, 2005).

Appendix

Appendix A—Paper Based Questionnaire for Studies 1, 2, and 4

Appendix A contains the questions from the paper based survey handed out to all students of a marketing class at a university in South Germany during a lecture used for Studies 1, 2, and 4. The four tariff choice situations amusement parks ("Fahrgeschäfte"), thermal bath visits ("Thermalbad"), public transportation ("Öffentlicher Personen Nahverkehr (ÖPNV)"), and dance lessons ("Tanzkurs") appeared in random order; showing only one of the three dance lesson variants (hedonic versus utilitarian versus hybrid).

Befragung zur Tarifwahl

Herzlichen Dank für Ihre Teilnahme an unserer Befragung zum Thema „Tarifwahl“! Die Daten werden im Rahmen einer Dissertation erhoben und dienen der wissenschaftlichen Forschung. Alle Antworten sind anonym – es gibt keine richtigen oder falschen Antworten. Antworten Sie bitte spontan und ohne langes Überlegen. Ziel der Umfrage ist es herauszufinden, in welchen Situationen Flat-Rate Tarife einem variablen Tarif vorgezogen werden und umgekehrt. Im Folgenden möchten wir Sie bitten, in den 4 vorgestellten Szenarien einen Tarif auszuwählen, und Ihre Entscheidung anhand diverser Fragen zu begründen. Die Bearbeitung dauert ca. 15 Minuten.

Soziodemographische Daten

- Wie alt sind Sie? ________ Jahre
- Ihr Geschlecht ist: O weiblich O männlich
- Ihre Nationalität: O Deutsch O andere: ________________

Tarifwahlsituation „Fahrgeschäfte"

Im folgenden Szenario geht es um die Nutzung von Fahrgeschäften wie bspw. Achterbahnen, Geisterbahnen und Karussellen gegen Gebühr. Bitte stellen Sie sich folgende Situation vor: Sie stehen am Eingang eines Vergnügungsparks und möchten sich ein Ticket kaufen.

Es stehen zwei Tarife zur Auswahl:

- Tarif 1: €3 pro Fahrt
  (zu zahlen beim Verlassen des Parks, Chip-Karte zeichnet die Anzahl der Fahrten auf)
- Tarif 2: Tageskarte für €24 (zu zahlen beim Verlassen des Parks, Chip-Karte berechtigt für beliebige Anzahl an Zutritten zu Fahrgeschäften)

Bitte nehmen Sie – unabhängig von Ihrer tatsächlichen Nutzung – folgendes historisches Verhalten an: Während den letzten Besuchen in diesem Vergnügungspark haben Sie durchschnittlich 8 Fahrten gemacht. Die Anzahl der Fahrten hat allerdings geschwankt – Ihr Minimum waren 4 Fahrten, Ihr Maximum waren 12 Fahrten.

Für welchen Tarif würden Sie sich entscheiden?

Definitiv Tarif 1 (€3 pro Fahrt)	Vermutlich Tarif 1 (€3 pro Fahrt)	Vermutlich Tarif 2 (Tageskarte: €24)	Definitiv Tarif 2 (Tageskarte: €24)

Bitte beschreiben Sie Ihre subjektive Einstellung ggü. den folgenden Aussagen…	Stimme absolut nicht zu	.	.	.	Stimme absolut zu
Eine Tageskarte für Fahrgeschäfte ist toll, weil ich nicht bei jeder Fahrt an die Kosten denke					
Für die Sicherheit, dass durch die Fahrten nie ein vereinbarter Preis überstiegen wird, zahle ich gegebenenfalls auch etwas mehr					
Es ist mir zu aufwendig, abzuschätzen, ob die Tageskarte oder pro Fahrt zu zahlen günstiger ist, bevor ich in den Vergnügungspark gehe					
Wenn ich eine Tageskarte habe, fühle ich mich freier und unbefangener in der Nutzung der Fahrgeschäfte als bei Bezahlung pro Fahrt					
Die Wahrscheinlichkeit, mehr Fahrten als sonst zu machen ist höher, als weniger zu machen					
Das Geld, das ich sparen kann, ist nicht die Zeit und den Aufwand wert, vor Betreten des Vergnügungsparks die Tarife zu studieren					
Ich kann mir gut vorstellen, mehr Fahrten mit Fahrgeschäften zu machen, als im Durchschnitt					
Auch wenn die Tageskarte für mich etwas teurer wäre als pro Fahrt zu zahlen, wäre ich zufrieden, weil meine Gesamtkosten nie einen vorher definierten Fixbetrag übersteigen					

Bitte beschreiben Sie Ihre subjektive Einstellung ggü. den folgenden Aussagen...	Stimme absolut nicht zu	.	.	.	Stimme absolut zu
Fahrgeschäfte fahren...					
...macht mir Spaß					
...finde ich aufregend					
...finde ich nützlich					
...ist spannend für mich					
...ist sinnvoll für mich					
...ist mir ein Vergnügen					
...ist zweckmäßig für mich					
...genieße ich					
...ist notwendig für mich					
...finde ich praktisch					

Nennen Sie uns bitte Ihr tatsächliches Nutzungsverhalten bzgl. Fahrgeschäfte.
Anzahl Fahrgeschäftsfahrten pro Jahr: ________

Tarifwahlsituation „Thermalbad"

Im folgenden Szenario geht es um den Besuch eines Thermalbads. Dieses bietet neben klassischen Schwimmbecken und Wasserrutschen auch eine Saunalandschaft mit Wellness- und Erholungsbereich. Bitte stellen Sie sich folgende Situation vor: Sie stehen vor der Kasse der Therme.

Es werden zwei Tarife angeboten:

- Tarif 1: €4 pro Stunde Besuchszeit
  (zu zahlen beim Verlassen des Thermalbads)
- Tarif 2: Tageskarte für €16
  (unbeschränkte Besuchsdauer, zu zahlen beim Verlassen des Thermalbads)

Bitte nehmen Sie – unabhängig von Ihrer tatsächlichen Nutzung – folgendes historisches Verhalten an: Während den letzten Thermalbad-Besuchen haben Sie durchschnittlich 4 Stunden Aufenthalt gehabt. Die Aufenthaltsdauer hat allerdings geschwankt – mindestens 2 Stunden, maximal 6 Stunden.

Für welchen Tarif würden Sie sich entscheiden?

Definitiv Tarif 1 (€4 pro Stunde)	Vermutlich Tarif 1 (€4 pro Stunde)	Vermutlich Tarif 2 (Tageskarte: €16)	Definitiv Tarif 2 (Tageskarte: €16)

Bitte beschreiben Sie Ihre subjektive Einstellung ggü. den folgenden Aussagen...	Stimme absolut nicht zu	.	.	.	Stimme absolut zu
Eine Tageskarte für die Therme ist toll, weil ich nicht jede Stunde an die Kosten denke					
Für die Sicherheit, dass durch den Thermenbesuch nie ein vereinbarter Preis überstiegen wird, zahle ich gegebenenfalls auch etwas mehr					
Es ist mir zu aufwendig, abzuschätzen, ob die Tageskarte oder pro Stunde zu zahlen günstiger für mich ist, bevor ich in die Therme gehe					
Wenn ich eine Tageskarte habe, fühle ich mich freier und unbefangener beim Besuch der Therme als bei einem variablen Tarif					
Die Wahrscheinlichkeit, mehr Zeit als sonst zu verbringen ist höher, als weniger zu verbringen					
Das Geld, das ich sparen kann, ist nicht die Zeit und den Aufwand wert, vor Betreten der Therme ausführlich die Tarife zu studieren					
Ich kann mir gut vorstellen, mehr Zeit in der Therme zu verbringen, als im Durchschnitt					
Auch wenn die Thermen-Tageskarte für mich etwas teurer wäre als pro Stunde zu zahlen, wäre ich zufrieden, weil meine Gesamtkosten nie einen vorher definierten Fixbetrag übersteigen					

Bitte beschreiben Sie Ihre subjektive Einstellung ggü. den folgenden Aussagen...	Stimme absolut nicht zu	.	.	.	Stimme absolut zu
In ein Thermalbad zu gehen...					
...macht mir Spaß					
...finde ich aufregend					
...finde ich nützlich					
...ist spannend für mich					
...ist sinnvoll für mich					
...ist mir ein Vergnügen					
...ist zweckmäßig für mich					
...genieße ich					
...ist notwendig für mich					
...finde ich praktisch					

Geben Sie bitte Ihr tatsächliches Nutzungsverhalten bzgl. Thermalbädern an...
Anzahl Thermenbesuche pro Jahr: ________

Tarifwahlsituation „Öffentlicher Personen Nah-Verkehr" (ÖPNV)

Im folgenden Szenario geht es um die Nutzung des Öffentlichen Personen Nah-Verkehrs. Dies beinhaltet U-Bahnen, S-Bahnen, Tram-Bahnen und Busse zum Transport gegen Gebühr. Bitte stellen Sie sich folgende Situation vor: Sie stehen an der U-Bahn Station und planen einige Erledigungen in der Stadt.

Es stehen Ihnen zwei Tarife zur Auswahl:

- Tarif 1: €2 pro Fahrt
  (Die Abbuchung erfolgt je Fahrt über eine zuvor aufgeladene Magnetkarte)
- Tarif 2: Tageskarte für €8
  (Eine Magnetkarte ermöglicht beliebig viele Fahrten an diesem Tag)

Bitte nehmen Sie – unabhängig von Ihrer tatsächlichen Nutzung – folgendes historisches Verhalten an: Während den letzten Erledigungen haben Sie durchschnittlich 4 Fahrten gemacht. Die Anzahl der Fahrten hat allerdings geschwankt – es waren mindestens 2 Fahrten, maximal 6 Fahrten.

Für welchen Tarif würden Sie sich entscheiden?

Definitiv Tarif 1 (€2 pro Fahrt)	Vermutlich Tarif 1 (€2 pro Fahrt)	Vermutlich Tarif 2 (Tageskarte für €8)	Definitiv Tarif 2 (Tageskarte für €8)

Bitte beschreiben Sie Ihre subjektive Einstellung ggü. den folgenden Aussagen...	Stimme absolut nicht zu	.	.	.	Stimme absolut zu
Eine Tageskarte für den ÖPNV ist toll, weil ich nicht bei jeder Fahrt an die Kosten denke					
Für die Sicherheit, dass durch die ÖPNV Fahrten nie ein vereinbarter Preis überstiegen wird, zahle ich gegebenenfalls auch etwas mehr					
Es ist mir zu aufwendig, abzuschätzen, ob die Tageskarte oder pro Fahrt zu zahlen günstiger für mich ist, bevor ich den ÖPNV nutze					
Wenn ich eine Tageskarte habe, fühle ich mich freier und unbefangener in der Nutzung des ÖPNV als bei einem variablen Tarif					
Die Wahrscheinlichkeit, mehr Fahrten als sonst mit dem ÖPNV zu machen ist höher, als die, weniger zu machen					
Das Geld, das ich sparen kann, ist nicht die Zeit und den Aufwand wert, vor Nutzung des ÖPNV ausführlich die Tarife zu studieren					
Ich kann mir gut vorstellen, mehr Fahrten mit dem ÖPNV zu machen, als im Durchschnitt					
Auch wenn die Tageskarte für mich etwas teurer wäre als pro Fahrt zu zahlen, wäre ich zufrieden, weil meine Gesamtkosten nie einen vorher definierten Fixbetrag übersteigen					

Mit dem ÖPNV zu fahren...					
...macht mir Spaß					
...finde ich aufregend					
...finde ich nützlich					
...ist spannend für mich					
...ist sinnvoll für mich					
...ist mir ein Vergnügen					
...ist zweckmäßig für mich					
...genieße ich					
...ist notwendig für mich					
...finde ich praktisch					

Geben Sie bitte Ihr tatsächliches Nutzungsverhalten bzgl. des Öffentlichen Personen Nah-Verkehrs an. Anzahl Nutzungstage pro Monat: ________

Tarifwahlsituation „Tanzkurs" (Hedonic)

Im folgenden Szenario geht es nicht um Sie, sondern um den fiktiven Charakter Andrea. Für Andrea ist Tanzen die große Leidenschaft – sie liebt es, sich im Rhythmus der Musik auf der Tanzfläche zu bewegen. Was ihre Fertigkeiten angeht, so beherrscht sie bereits alle Schritte perfekt. Um dieses Hobby weiter auszuüben, erwägt sie einen weiteren Tanzkurs zu besuchen – nicht, weil sie dadurch etwas Neues lernen könnte, sondern nur zum Spaß.

Andreas Tanzschule bietet ihr die folgenden zwei Tarife an:

- Tarif 1: €15 pro Tanzstunde
  (zu zahlen am Quartalsende)
- Tarif 2: Quartalskarte für €150
  (beliebig viele Tanzstunden im Quartal, zu zahlen am Quartalsende)

Andrea geht im Durchschnitt 10-mal im Quartal tanzen – mindestens aber 7-mal, maximal 13-mal.

Für welchen Tarif würden sich Andrea entscheiden?

Definitiv Tarif 1 (€15 pro Tanzstunde)	Vermutlich Tarif 1 (€15 pro Tanzstunde)	Vermutlich Tarif 2 (Quartalskarte €150)	Definitiv Tarif 2 (Quartalskarte €150)

Bitte beschreiben Sie Andreas Einstellung ggü. den folgenden Aussagen...	Stimme absolut nicht zu	.	.	.	Stimme absolut zu
Eine Quartalskarte für die Tanzschule ist toll, weil Andrea nicht bei jeder Tanzstunde an die Kosten denkt					
Für die Sicherheit, dass durch die Tanzstunden nie ein vereinbarter Preis überstiegen wird, zahlt Andrea gegebenenfalls auch etwas mehr					
Es ist zu aufwendig für Andrea, abzuschätzen, ob die Quartalskarte oder pro Tanzstunde zu zahlen günstiger für sie ist					
Wenn Andrea eine Quartalskarte hat, fühlt sie sich freier und unbefangener bei der Nutzung der Tanzschule als bei einem variablen Tarif					
Die Wahrscheinlichkeit, dass Andrea mehr Tanzstunden als sonst macht ist höher, als die, dass sie weniger macht					
Das Geld, das Andrea sparen kann, ist nicht die Zeit und den Aufwand wert, ausführlich die Tarife zu studieren					
Andrea kann sich gut vorstellen, mehr Tanzstunden zu machen, als im Durchschnitt					
Auch wenn die Quartalskarte für Andrea etwas teurer wäre als pro Tanzstunde zu zahlen, wäre sie zufrieden, weil ihre Gesamtkosten nie einen vorher					

Bitte beschreiben Sie Andreas Einstellung ggü. den folgenden Aussagen...	Stimme absolut nicht zu	.	.	.	Stimme absolut zu
definierten Fixbetrag übersteigen					
Tanzen...					
...macht Andrea Spaß					
...findet Andrea aufregend					
...findet Andrea nützlich					
...ist spannend für Andrea					
...ist sinnvoll für Andrea					
...ist Andrea ein Vergnügen					
...ist zweckmäßig für Andrea					
...genießt Andrea					
...ist notwendig für Andrea					
...findet Andrea praktisch					

Geben Sie bitte Ihr eigenes tatsächliches Nutzungsverhalten bzgl. Tanzen an…
Anzahl Tanzstunden im Jahr: ________

Tarifwahlsituation „Tanzkurs" (Hybrid)

Im folgenden Szenario geht es nicht um Sie, sondern um den fiktiven Charakter Susanne. Susanne möchte einen Tanzkurs buchen, um Ihre Salsa-Fertigkeiten weiterzuentwickeln. Susanne liebt Tanzen über alles und hat großen Spaß daran, neue Schritte zu lernen und ihr Niveau zu steigern.

Susannes Tanzschule bietet ihr die folgenden zwei Tarife an:

- Tarif 1: €15 pro Tanzstunde
  (zu zahlen am Quartalsende)
- Tarif 2: Quartalskarte für €150
  (beliebig viele Tanzstunden im Quartal, zu zahlen am Quartalsende)

Susanne geht im Durchschnitt 10-mal im Quartal tanzen – mindestens aber 7-mal, maximal 13-mal.

Für welchen Tarif würden sich Susanne entscheiden?

Definitiv Tarif 1 (€15 pro Tanzstunde)	Vermutlich Tarif 1 (€15 pro Tanzstunde)	Vermutlich Tarif 2 (Quartalskarte €150)	Definitiv Tarif 2 (Quartalskarte €150)

Bitte beschreiben Sie Susannes Einstellung ggü. den folgenden Aussagen...	Stimme absolut nicht zu	.	.	.	Stimme absolut zu
Eine Quartalskarte für die Tanzschule ist toll, weil Susanne nicht bei jeder Tanzstunde an die Kosten denkt					
Für die Sicherheit, dass durch die Tanzstunden nie ein vereinbarter Preis überstiegen wird, zahlt Susanne gegebenenfalls auch etwas mehr					
Es ist zu aufwendig für Susanne, abzuschätzen, ob die Quartalskarte oder pro Tanzstunde zu zahlen günstiger für sie ist					
Wenn Susanne eine Quartalskarte hat, fühlt sie sich freier und unbefangener bei der Nutzung der Tanzschule als bei einem variablen Tarif					
Die Wahrscheinlichkeit, dass Susanne mehr Tanzstunden als sonst macht ist höher, als die, dass sie weniger macht					
Das Geld, das Susanne sparen kann, ist nicht die Zeit und den Aufwand wert, ausführlich die Tarife zu studieren					
Susanne kann sich gut vorstellen, mehr Tanzstunden zu machen, als im Durchschnitt					
Auch wenn die Quartalskarte für Susanne etwas teurer wäre als pro Tanzstunde zu zahlen, wäre sie zufrieden, weil ihre Gesamtkosten nie einen vorher definierten Fixbetrag übersteigen					

Bitte beschreiben Sie Susannes Einstellung ggü. den folgenden Aussagen...	Stimme absolut nicht zu	.	.	.	Stimme absolut zu
Tanzen...					
...macht Susanne Spaß					
...findet Susanne aufregend					
...findet Susanne nützlich					
...ist spannend für Susanne					
...ist sinnvoll für Susanne					
...ist Susanne ein Vergnügen					
...ist zweckmäßig für Susanne					
...genießt Susanne					
...ist notwendig für Susanne					
...findet Susanne praktisch					

Geben Sie bitte Ihr eigenes tatsächliches Nutzungsverhalten bzgl. Tanzen an...
Anzahl Tanzstunden im Jahr: ________

Tarifwahlsituation „Tanzkurs" (Utilitarian)

Im folgenden Szenario geht es nicht um Sie, sondern um den fiktiven Charakter Daniel. Daniel steht dem Tanzen eher skeptisch gegenüber. Er kann es nicht besonders gut und es macht ihm keinen Spaß. Allerdings ist er zum Jahresende auf einem Ball eingeladen. Um dort einen guten Eindruck zu hinterlassen, will er einen Tanzkurs besuchen, in dem er die wichtigsten Schritte lernt.

Die Tanzschule bietet ihm die folgenden zwei Tarife an:

- Tarif 1: €15 pro Tanzstunde
  (zu zahlen am Quartalsende)
- Tarif 2: Quartalskarte für €150
  (beliebig viele Tanzstunden im Quartal, zu zahlen am Quartalsende)

Daniel hat genau ein Quartal Zeit. Die Tanzschule erklärt Daniel, dass Tänzer für sein Lernziel üblicherweise 10 Trainingseinheiten im Quartal benötigen – manchmal mehr, manchmal weniger. Mindestens sind es aber 7 Tanzstunden, maximal 13 Tanzstunden.

Für welchen Tarif würde sich Daniel entscheiden?

Definitiv Tarif 1 (€15 pro Tanzstunde)	Vermutlich Tarif 1 (€15 pro Tanzstunde)	Vermutlich Tarif 2 (Quartalskarte €150)	Definitiv Tarif 2 (Quartalskarte €150)

Bitte beschreiben Sie Daniels Einstellung ggü. den folgenden Aussagen...	Stimme absolut nicht zu	.	.	.	Stimme absolut zu
Eine Quartalskarte für die Tanzschule ist toll, weil Daniel nicht bei jeder Tanzstunde an die Kosten denkt					
Für die Sicherheit, dass durch die Tanzstunden nie ein vereinbarter Preis überstiegen wird, zahlt Daniel gegebenenfalls auch etwas mehr					
Es ist zu aufwendig für Daniel, abzuschätzen, ob die Quartalskarte oder pro Tanzstunde zu zahlen günstiger für ihn ist					
Wenn Daniel eine Quartalskarte hat, fühlt er sich freier und unbefangener bei der Nutzung der Tanzschule als bei einem variablen Tarif					
Die Wahrscheinlichkeit, dass Daniel mehr Tanzstunden als sonst macht ist höher, als die, dass er weniger macht					
Das Geld, das Daniel sparen kann, ist nicht die Zeit und den Aufwand wert, ausführlich die Tarife zu studieren					
Daniel kann sich gut vorstellen, mehr Tanzstunden zu machen, als im Durchschnitt					
Auch wenn die Quartalskarte für Daniel etwas teurer wäre als pro Tanzstunde zu zahlen, wäre er zufrieden, weil seine Gesamtkosten nie einen vorher definierten Fixbetrag übersteigen					

Bitte beschreiben Sie Daniels Einstellung ggü. den folgenden Aussagen...	Stimme absolut nicht zu	.	.	.	Stimme absolut zu
Tanzen...					
...macht Daniel Spaß					
...findet Daniel aufregend					
...findet Daniel nützlich					
...ist spannend für Daniel					
...ist sinnvoll für Daniel					
...ist Daniel ein Vergnügen					
...ist zweckmäßig für Daniel					
...genießt Daniel					
...ist notwendig für Daniel					
...findet Daniel praktisch					

Geben Sie bitte Ihr eigenes tatsächliches Nutzungsverhalten bzgl. Tanzen an...
Anzahl Tanzstunden im Jahr: ________

Appendix B—Online Survey for Study 3

Appendix B contains the questions from the online questionnaire used for Study 3 and distributed by the marketing research agency Research Now. Only one of the three scenarios (hedonic versus utilitarian versus hybrid) appeared to the respondent by random selection.

Einleitung

Herzlichen Dank für die Teilnahme an der Umfrage zum Thema Tarifwahl!
Die Daten werden im Rahmen einer Dissertation erhoben und dienen der wissenschaftlichen Forschung. Alle Antworten sind anonym – es gibt keine richtigen oder falschen Antworten. Antworten Sie bitte spontan und ohne langes Überlegen.
Im Folgenden möchten wir Sie bitten, im vorgestellten Szenario einen Tarif auszuwählen und Ihre Entscheidung anhand diverser Fragen zu begründen. Die Bearbeitung des Fragebogens dauert ca. 10 Minuten.

Soziodemographie

Bitte nennen Sie uns Ihr Alter: ________
Was ist Ihr Geschlecht? O Männlich O Weiblich

Bitte geben Sie das ungefähres monatliche Bruttoeinkommen Ihres Haushalts an

- unter €1.500
- €1.500 bis €2.499
- €2.500 bis €3.499
- €3.500 bis €4.499
- €4.500 bis €5.499
- €5.500 bis €6.499
- €6.500 bis €7.499
- €7.500 oder mehr

Was ist Ihr höchster Bildungsabschluss?

- Kein Schulabschluss
- Volks- / Hauptschulabschluss
- Mittlere Reife / Realschule
- Abitur oder Fachhochschulreife
- Universitäts- oder Fachholschulabschluss
- Promotion / Habilitation

Thermalbad (Hedonic)

Im folgenden Szenario geht es nicht um Sie, sondern um einen fiktiven Charakter. Andrea liebt Thermalbäder. Einerseits genießt sie die Ruhe, entspannt im warmen Becken zu liegen, andererseits findet sie die Wasserrutschen ein spannendes und aufregendes Vergnügen. Allerdings hat sie manchmal schon ein schlechtes Gewissen, denn es ist weder sinnvoll, noch nützlich. Und wirklich notwendig ist das Thermalbad für sie auch nicht – es macht einfach nur Spaß!

Für welchen Tarif wird sich Andrea bei ihrem nächsten Besuch entscheiden, wenn die folgenden Tarife angeboten werden?

- Tarif 1: €4 je Stunde Besuchszeit
  (zu zahlen am Ende des Besuchs basierend auf der tatsächlichen Besuchsdauer)
- Tarif 2: Tageskarte für €16
  (unbeschränkte Besuchsdauer)

Die letzten Male hat Andrea mindestens 2 Stunden, im Durchschnitt 4 Stunden, und maximal 6 Stunden im Thermalbad verbracht. Bitte versuchen Sie - unabhängig von ihrem eigenem Nutzungsverhalten - eine Entscheidung aus der Perspektive von Andrea zu treffen.

Definitiv Tarif 1 (€4 pro Stunde)	Vermutlich Tarif 1 (€4 pro Stunde)	Vermutlich Tarif 2 (Tageskarte: €16)	Definitiv Tarif 2 (Tageskarte: €16)

Bitte beschreiben Sie Andreas Einstellung gegenüber den folgenden Aussagen...	Trifft absolut nicht zu	.	.	.	Trifft absolut zu
Die Tageskarte für das Thermalbad ist toll, weil Andrea nicht jede Stunde an die Kosten denken muss					
Andrea hat weniger Spaß im Thermalbad, wenn mit jeder Stunde die Kosten steigen					
Nur wenn Andrea eine Tageskarte hat, hat sie richtig Spaß im Thermalbad					
Wenn Andrea eine Tageskarte hat, fühlt sie sich viel freier und unbefangener beim Besuch des Thermalbads als bei einem variablen Tarif					
Die Vorstellung, dass mit jeder Stunde die Kosten steigen, stört Andrea					
Für die Sicherheit, dass ihr Thermalbadbesuch nie einen vereinbarten Preis übersteigen wird, zahlt Andrea gegebenenfalls auch etwas mehr					
Auch wenn die Tageskarte etwas teurer sein sollte als pro Stunde zu zahlen, wäre Andrea zufrieden, weil ihre Gesamtkosten nie einen vorher definierten Fixbetrag übersteigen					
Die Transparenz, vorab genau zu wissen, wieviel der Thermalbadbesuch kosten wird, ist Andrea wichtig					
Andrea ist es wichtig, dass durch den					

Bitte beschreiben Sie Andreas Einstellung gegenüber den folgenden Aussagen...	Trifft absolut nicht zu	.	.	.	Trifft absolut zu
Thermalbadbesuch nie ein vereinbarter Zahl-Betrag überschritten wird					
Andrea mag es nicht, wenn durch die Nutzung ein vorher definierter Preis überschritten wird					
Es ist Andrea viel zu aufwendig abzuschätzen, ob die Tageskarte oder pro Stunde zu zahlen günstiger ist					
Das Geld, das Andrea mit dem richtigen Tarif sparen kann, ist nicht die Zeit und den Aufwand wert, ausführlich die Tarife zu studieren					
So lange wie es dauert zu berechnen welcher Tarif günstiger ist, lohnt sich der Aufwand normalerweise nicht					
Andrea kann sich gut vorstellen, mehr Zeit im Thermalbad zu verbringen als im Durchschnitt					
Die Wahrscheinlichkeit, dass Andrea mehr Zeit im Thermalbad verbringt als normal ist höher als die, dass sie weniger Zeit verbringt					
Der Fall, dass Andrea das Thermalbad länger besucht, tritt eher ein als der Fall, dass sie es kürzer besucht					
Das Risiko, das Thermalbad länger als im Durchschnitt zu besuchen ist größer als das Risiko, das Thermalbad kürzer zu besuchen					
In ein Thermalbad zu gehen...					
...macht Andrea Spaß					
...findet Andrea aufregend					
...genießt Andrea					
...ist spannend für Andrea					
...ist Andrea ein Vergnügen					
...ist sinnvoll für Andrea					
...findet Andrea nützlich					
...ist zweckmäßig für Andrea					
...ist notwendig für Andrea					
...findet Andrea praktisch					

Thermalbad (Utilitarian)

Im folgenden Szenario geht es nicht um Sie, sondern um einen fiktiven Charakter. Für Andrea ist der Besuch im Thermalbad kein Genuss. Aber für Ihr Rheuma-Leiden sind die Mineralstoffe absolut notwendig. Das Baden im heißen Thermalwasser ist für ihre Gesundheit sinnvoll und zweckmäßig, um die Mineralstoffkonzentration in ihrem Körper zu steigern. Also eine sehr praktische und nützliche Art, die Schmerzen zu lindern - auch wenn Sie keinen großen Spaß oder Vergnügen dabei hat.

Für welchen Tarif wird sich Andrea bei ihrem nächsten Besuch entscheiden, wenn die folgenden Tarife angeboten werden?

- Tarif 1: €4 je Stunde Besuchszeit
  (zu zahlen am Ende des Besuchs basierend auf der tatsächlichen Besuchsdauer)
- Tarif 2: Tageskarte für €16
  (unbeschränkte Besuchsdauer)

Die letzten Male hat Andrea mindestens 2 Stunden, im Durchschnitt 4 Stunden, und maximal 6 Stunden im Thermalbad verbracht. Bitte versuchen Sie - unabhängig von ihrem eigenem Nutzungsverhalten - eine Entscheidung aus der Perspektive von Andrea zu treffen.

Definitiv Tarif 1 (€4 pro Stunde)	Vermutlich Tarif 1 (€4 pro Stunde)	Vermutlich Tarif 2 (Tageskarte: €16)	Definitiv Tarif 2 (Tageskarte: €16)

Bitte beschreiben Sie Andreas Einstellung gegenüber den folgenden Aussagen...	Trifft absolut nicht zu	.	.	.	Trifft absolut zu
Die Tageskarte für das Thermalbad ist toll, weil Andrea nicht jede Stunde an die Kosten denken muss					
Andrea hat weniger Spaß im Thermalbad, wenn mit jeder Stunde die Kosten steigen					
Nur wenn Andrea eine Tageskarte hat, hat sie richtig Spaß im Thermalbad					
Wenn Andrea eine Tageskarte hat, fühlt sie sich viel freier und unbefangener beim Besuch des Thermalbads als bei einem variablen Tarif					
Die Vorstellung, dass mit jeder Stunde die Kosten steigen, stört Andrea					
Für die Sicherheit, dass ihr Thermalbadbesuch nie einen vereinbarten Preis übersteigen wird, zahlt Andrea gegebenenfalls auch etwas mehr					
Auch wenn die Tageskarte etwas teurer sein sollte als pro Stunde zu zahlen, wäre Andrea zufrieden, weil ihre Gesamtkosten nie einen vorher definierten Fixbetrag übersteigen					
Die Transparenz, vorab genau zu wissen, wieviel der Thermalbadbesuch kosten wird, ist Andrea wichtig					

Bitte beschreiben Sie Andreas Einstellung gegenüber den folgenden Aussagen...	Trifft absolut nicht zu	.	.	.	Trifft absolut zu
Andrea ist es wichtig, dass durch den Thermalbadbesuch nie ein vereinbarter Zahl-Betrag überschritten wird					
Andrea mag es nicht, wenn durch die Nutzung ein vorher definierter Preis überschritten wird					
Es ist Andrea viel zu aufwendig abzuschätzen, ob die Tageskarte oder pro Stunde zu zahlen günstiger ist					
Das Geld, das Andrea mit dem richtigen Tarif sparen kann, ist nicht die Zeit und den Aufwand wert, ausführlich die Tarife zu studieren					
So lange wie es dauert zu berechnen welcher Tarif günstiger ist, lohnt sich der Aufwand normalerweise nicht					
Andrea kann sich gut vorstellen, mehr Zeit im Thermalbad zu verbringen als im Durchschnitt					
Die Wahrscheinlichkeit, dass Andrea mehr Zeit im Thermalbad verbringt als normal ist höher als die, dass sie weniger Zeit verbringt					
Der Fall, dass Andrea das Thermalbad länger besucht, tritt eher ein als der Fall, dass sie es kürzer besucht					
Das Risiko, das Thermalbad länger als im Durchschnitt zu besuchen ist größer als das Risiko, das Thermalbad kürzer zu besuchen					
In ein Thermalbad zu gehen...					
...macht Andrea Spaß					
...findet Andrea aufregend					
...genießt Andrea					
...ist spannend für Andrea					
...ist Andrea ein Vergnügen					
...ist sinnvoll für Andrea					
...findet Andrea nützlich					
...ist zweckmäßig für Andrea					
...ist notwendig für Andrea					
...findet Andrea praktisch					

Thermalbad (Hybrid)

Im folgenden Szenario geht es nicht um Sie, sondern um einen fiktiven Charakter. Andrea liebt Thermalbäder. Zuerst hat Sie großen Spaß an den spannended und aufregended Wasserrutschen. Anschließend genießt Sie die Ruhe im Entspannungsbereich. Diese Kombination ist für Andrea sehr praktisch und nützlich, da sie nur so die notwendige Ablenkung von der Arbeit bekommt. Außerdem ist das mineralstoffhaltige Thermalwasser sinnvoll für sie, um eine schöne Haut zu bekommen.

Für welchen Tarif wird sich Andrea bei ihrem nächsten Besuch entscheiden, wenn die folgenden Tarife angeboten werden?

- Tarif 1: €4 je Stunde Besuchszeit
  (zu zahlen am Ende des Besuchs basierend auf der tatsächlichen Besuchsdauer)
- Tarif 2: Tageskarte für €16
  (unbeschränkte Besuchsdauer)

Die letzten Male hat Andrea mindestens 2 Stunden, im Durchschnitt 4 Stunden, und maximal 6 Stunden im Thermalbad verbracht. Bitte versuchen Sie - unabhängig von ihrem eigenem Nutzungsverhalten - eine Entscheidung aus der Perspektive von Andrea zu treffen.

Definitiv Tarif 1 (€4 pro Stunde)	Vermutlich Tarif 1 (€4 pro Stunde)	Vermutlich Tarif 2 (Tageskarte: €16)	Definitiv Tarif 2 (Tageskarte: €16)

Bitte beschreiben Sie Andreas Einstellung gegenüber den folgenden Aussagen...	Trifft absolut nicht zu	.	.	.	Trifft absolut zu
Die Tageskarte für das Thermalbad ist toll, weil Andrea nicht jede Stunde an die Kosten denken muss					
Andrea hat weniger Spaß im Thermalbad, wenn mit jeder Stunde die Kosten steigen					
Nur wenn Andrea eine Tageskarte hat, hat sie richtig Spaß im Thermalbad					
Wenn Andrea eine Tageskarte hat, fühlt sie sich viel freier und unbefangener beim Besuch des Thermalbads als bei einem variablen Tarif					
Die Vorstellung, dass mit jeder Stunde die Kosten steigen, stört Andrea					
Für die Sicherheit, dass ihr Thermalbadbesuch nie einen vereinbarten Preis übersteigen wird, zahlt Andrea gegebenenfalls auch etwas mehr					
Auch wenn die Tageskarte etwas teurer sein sollte als pro Stunde zu zahlen, wäre Andrea zufrieden, weil ihre Gesamtkosten nie einen vorher definierten Fixbetrag übersteigen					
Die Transparenz, vorab genau zu wissen, wieviel der					

Bitte beschreiben Sie Andreas Einstellung gegenüber den folgenden Aussagen...	Trifft absolut nicht zu	.	.	.	Trifft absolut zu
Thermalbadbesuch kosten wird, ist Andrea wichtig					
Andrea ist es wichtig, dass durch den Thermalbadbesuch nie ein vereinbarter Zahl-Betrag überschritten wird					
Andrea mag es nicht, wenn durch die Nutzung ein vorher definierter Preis überschritten wird					
Es ist Andrea viel zu aufwendig abzuschätzen, ob die Tageskarte oder pro Stunde zu zahlen günstiger ist					
Das Geld, das Andrea mit dem richtigen Tarif sparen kann, ist nicht die Zeit und den Aufwand wert, ausführlich die Tarife zu studieren					
So lange wie es dauert zu berechnen welcher Tarif günstiger ist, lohnt sich der Aufwand normalerweise nicht					
Andrea kann sich gut vorstellen, mehr Zeit im Thermalbad zu verbringen als im Durchschnitt					
Die Wahrscheinlichkeit, dass Andrea mehr Zeit im Thermalbad verbringt als normal ist höher als die, dass sie weniger Zeit verbringt					
Der Fall, dass Andrea das Thermalbad länger besucht, tritt eher ein als der Fall, dass sie es kürzer besucht					
Das Risiko, das Thermalbad länger als im Durchschnitt zu besuchen ist größer als das Risiko, das Thermalbad kürzer zu besuchen					
In ein Thermalbad zu gehen...					
...macht Andrea Spaß					
...findet Andrea aufregend					
...genießt Andrea					
...ist spannend für Andrea					
...ist Andrea ein Vergnügen					
...ist sinnvoll für Andrea					
...findet Andrea nützlich					
...ist zweckmäßig für Andrea					
...ist notwendig für Andrea					
...findet Andrea praktisch					

Appendix C—Online Survey for Study 5

Appendix C contains the questions from the online survey used for Study 5 and conducted by the research agency Research Now.

Einleitung

Herzlichen Dank für die Teilnahme an der Umfrage zum Thema Tarifwahl!
Die Daten werden im Rahmen einer Dissertation der Technischen Universität München erhoben und dienen der wissenschaftlichen Forschung. Alle Antworten sind anonym – es gibt keine richtigen oder falschen Antworten. Antworten Sie bitte spontan und ohne langes Überlegen.
Im Folgenden möchten wir Sie bitten, im vorgestellten Szenario einen Tarif auszuwählen und Ihre Entscheidung anhand diverser Fragen zu begründen. Die Bearbeitung des Fragebogens dauert ca. 5 Minuten.

Soziodemografie

Bitte nennen Sie uns Ihr Alter: _______
Was ist Ihr Geschlecht? O Männlich O Weiblich

Bitte geben Sie das ungefähre monatliche Nettoeinkommen Ihres Haushalts an

- unter €1.000
- €1.000 bis €1.499
- €1.500 bis €1.999
- €2.000 bis €2.499
- €2.500 bis €2.999
- €3.000 oder mehr

Was ist Ihr höchster Bildungsabschluss?

- maximal Hauptschulabschluss
- Mittlere Reife
- Abitur (ohne Universitätsabschluss)
- Studium

Energie Museum

Bitte stellen Sie sich vor, Sie wären auf einer Städtereise. Dort gibt es ein „Energie-Museum“, das Sie besuchen möchten.

Das Museum präsentiert das Thema Energie ganzheitlich - von der Gewinnung zum Verbrauch. Ein spezieller Fokus liegt dabei auf dem Trend des Energiesparens. Im Museum befinden sich zahlreiche Schautafeln, auf denen Wissen zum Energiesparen vermittelt wird. Aber auch diverse technische Geräte, an denen das neu erlernte Wissen ausprobiert werden kann.

Am Eingang haben Sie die Wahl zwischen folgenden Tarifen:

- Tarif 1: €4 je Stunde Besuchszeit
  (zu zahlen am Ende des Besuchs basierend auf der tatsächlichen Besuchsdauer)
- Tarif 2: Tageskarte für €12
  (unbeschränkte Besuchsdauer)

Für welchen Tarif würden Sie sich entscheiden?
Ihr Reiseführer empfiehlt: „Für den Besuch des Energie-Museums sollten Sie mindestens 1 Stunde einplanen. Die meisten Besucher brauchen im Schnitt 3 Stunden – maximal 5 Stunden sollten ausreichen.“

Definitiv Tarif 1 (€4 pro Stunde)	Vermutlich Tarif 1 (€4 pro Stunde)	Vermutlich Tarif 2 (Tageskarte: €12)	Definitiv Tarif 2 (Tageskarte: €12)

Bitte beschreiben Sie Ihre subjektive Einstellung gegenüber den folgenden Aussagen…	Trifft absolut nicht zu	.	.	.	Trifft absolut zu
Die Tageskarte für das Energie-Museum ist toll, weil ich nicht jede Stunde an die Kosten denken muss					
Ich habe weniger Spaß im Energie-Museum, wenn mit jeder Stunde die Kosten steigen					
Nur, wenn ich eine Tageskarte habe, habe ich richtig Spaß am Energie-Museum					
Wenn ich eine Tageskarte habe, fühle ich mich viel freier und unbefangener beim Besuch des Energie-Museums als bei einem variablen Tarif					
Die Vorstellung, dass mit jeder Stunde die Kosten steigen, stört mich					
Für die Sicherheit, dass mein Museumsbesuch nie einen vereinbarten Preis übersteigen wird, zahle ich gegebenenfalls auch etwas mehr					
Auch wenn die Tageskarte etwas teurer sein sollte als pro Stunde zu zahlen, wäre ich zufrieden, weil meine Gesamtkosten nie einen vorher definierten Fixbetrag übersteigen					
Die Transparenz, vorab genau zu wissen, wieviel der					

Bitte beschreiben Sie Ihre subjektive Einstellung gegenüber den folgenden Aussagen...	Trifft absolut nicht zu	.	.	.	Trifft absolut zu
Museumsbesuch kosten wird, ist mir wichtig					
Mir ist es wichtig, dass durch den Museumsbesuch nie ein vereinbarter Zahl-Betrag überschritten wird					
Ich mag es nicht, wenn durch die Nutzung ein vorher definierter Preis überschritten wird					
Es ist mir viel zu aufwendig abzuschätzen, ob die Tageskarte oder pro Stunde zu zahlen günstiger ist					
Das Geld, das ich mit dem richtigen Tarif sparen kann, ist nicht die Zeit und den Aufwand wert, ausführlich die Tarife zu studieren					
So lange wie es dauert zu berechnen welcher Tarif günstiger ist, lohnt sich der Aufwand normalerweise nicht					
Ich kann mir gut vorstellen, mehr Zeit im Energie-Museum zu verbringen als im Durchschnitt					
Die Wahrscheinlichkeit, dass ich mehr Zeit im Energie-Museum verbringe als normal ist höher als die, dass ich weniger Zeit verbringe					
Der Fall, dass ich das Energie-Museum länger besuche, tritt eher ein, als der Fall, dass ich es kürzer besuche					
Das Risiko, das Energie-Museum länger als im Durchschnitt zu besuchen, ist größer als das Risiko, das Energie-Museum kürzer zu besuchen					
Das Energie-Museum zu besuchen...					
...wird mir Spaß machen					
...finde ich aufregend					
...werde ich genießen					
...finde ich spannend					
...wird mir ein Vergnügen sein					
...ist sinnvoll für mich					
...empfinde ich als nützlich für mich					
...ist zweckmäßig für mich					
...erachte ich als notwendig für mich					
...wird praktisch für mich sein					

Appendix D—Online Survey for Study 6

Appendix D contains the questions from the online questionnaire used for Study 6, conducted among friends and family. Only one of the three scenarios (hedonic versus utilitarian versus hybrid) appeared to the respondent by random selection.

Einleitung

Herzlichen Dank für die Teilnahme an der Umfrage zum Thema Tarifwahl!
Die Daten werden im Rahmen einer Dissertation der Technischen Universität München erhoben und dienen der wissenschaftlichen Forschung. Alle Antworten sind anonym – es gibt keine richtigen oder falschen Antworten. Antworten Sie bitte spontan und ohne langes Überlegen.

Im Folgenden möchten wir Sie bitten, in dem vorgestellten Szenario einen Tarif auszuwählen und Ihre Entscheidung anhand der folgenden Fragen zu begründen. Die Bearbeitung des Fragebogens dauert ca. 2 Minuten.

Thermalbad (Hedonic)

[The specific stimuli used in this study are available from the author upon request]

Bitte schauen Sie sich die Werbeanzeige oben in Ruhe an. Anschließend bitten wir Sie, einige Fragen zu beantworten. Denken Sie dabei bitte nicht an andere, Ihnen bekannte Badeanstalten, sondern versuchen Sie, die Fragen immer in Bezug zur oben beworbenen Badeanstalt zu beantworten.

Wie viel wären Sie bereit, für einen Besuch der Badeanstalt zu zahlen?
Bitte geben Sie je einen Euro Betrag für die zwei möglichen Tarife an.

- Für eine Tageskarte (€ pro Tag): ______
- Pro Stunde Besuchszeit (€ pro Stunde): ______

Für welchen Tarif würden Sie sich entscheiden?

Definitiv "pro Stunde"	Vermutlich "pro Stunde"	Vermutlich "Tageskarte"	Definitiv "Tageskarte"

In die Badeanstalt zu gehen...	Trifft absolut nicht zu	.	.	.	Trifft absolut zu
...wird mir Spaß machen					
...werde ich aufregend finden					
...werde ich genießen					
...werde ich spannend finden					
...wird mir ein Vergnügen sein					
...halte ich für sinnvoll					
...finde ich nützlich					
...ist zweckmäßig für mich					
...ist notwendig für mich					
...finde ich praktisch					

Wie finden Sie die Anzeige oben?

Schlecht						Gut
Nicht ansprechend						Ansprechend
Langweilig						Interessant
Nicht kreativ						Kreativ
Nicht informativ						Informativ

Thermalbad (Utilitarian)

[The specific stimuli used in this study are available from the author upon request]

Bitte schauen Sie sich die Werbeanzeige oben in Ruhe an. Anschließend bitten wir Sie, einige Fragen zu beantworten. Denken Sie dabei bitte nicht an andere, Ihnen bekannte Badeanstalten, sondern versuchen Sie, die Fragen immer in Bezug zur oben beworbenen Badeanstalt zu beantworten.

Wie viel wären Sie bereit, für einen Besuch der Badeanstalt zu zahlen?
Bitte geben Sie je einen Euro Betrag für die zwei möglichen Tarife an.

- Für eine Tageskarte (€ pro Tag): ______
- Pro Stunde Besuchszeit (€ pro Stunde): ______

Für welchen Tarif würden Sie sich entscheiden?

Definitiv "pro Stunde"	Vermutlich "pro Stunde"	Vermutlich "Tageskarte"	Definitiv "Tageskarte"

In die Badeanstalt zu gehen...	Trifft absolut nicht zu	.	.	.	Trifft absolut zu
...wird mir Spaß machen					
...werde ich aufregend finden					
...werde ich genießen					
...werde ich spannend finden					
...wird mir ein Vergnügen sein					
...halte ich für sinnvoll					
...finde ich nützlich					
...ist zweckmäßig für mich					
...ist notwendig für mich					
...finde ich praktisch					

Wie finden Sie die Anzeige oben?

Schlecht						Gut
Nicht ansprechend						Ansprechend
Langweilig						Interessant
Nicht kreativ						Kreativ
Nicht informative						Informativ

Thermalbad (Hybrid)

[The specific stimuli used in this study are available from the author upon request]

Bitte schauen Sie sich die Werbeanzeige oben in Ruhe an. Anschließend bitten wir Sie, einige Fragen zu beantworten. Denken Sie dabei bitte nicht an andere, Ihnen bekannte Badeanstalten, sondern versuchen Sie, die Fragen immer in Bezug zur oben beworbenen Badeanstalt zu beantworten.

Wie viel wären Sie bereit, für einen Besuch der Badeanstalt zu zahlen?
Bitte geben Sie je einen Euro Betrag für die zwei möglichen Tarife an.

- Für eine Tageskarte (€ pro Tag): ______
- Pro Stunde Besuchszeit (€ pro Stunde): ______

Für welchen Tarif würden Sie sich entscheiden?

Definitiv "pro Stunde"	Vermutlich "pro Stunde"	Vermutlich "Tageskarte"	Definitiv "Tageskarte"

In die Badeanstalt zu gehen...	Trifft absolut nicht zu	.	.	.	Trifft absolut zu
...wird mir Spaß machen					
...werde ich aufregend finden					
...werde ich genießen					
...werde ich spannend finden					
...wird mir ein Vergnügen sein					
...halte ich für sinnvoll					
...finde ich nützlich					
...ist zweckmäßig für mich					
...ist notwendig für mich					
...finde ich praktisch					

Wie finden Sie die Anzeige oben?

Schlecht					Gut
Nicht ansprechend					Ansprechend
Langweilig					Interessant
Nicht kreativ					Kreativ
Nicht informativ					Informativ

Appendix E—Online Survey for Study 8

Appendix G contains the questions from the online survey conducted among friends and family. Only one of the three scenarios (Reale Kunden versus PrimeTel versus GünsTel) was shown to the respondents by random selection.

Einleitung

In der Befragung geht es primär um das Thema Sprachtelefonie. Versuchen Sie bitte andere Services wie SMS und Mobile Data geistig auszublenden.

Für Sprachtelefonie werden auf den folgenden Seiten drei Tarife unterschieden:

- Pay-Per-Use = Nutzungsabhängiges Entgelt (Euro pro Minute) mit oder ohne monatlicher Grundgebühr (beinhaltet auch Tarife mit sogenanntem Kostenschutz /-airbag). Bspw. "11 Cent pro Minute in alle Netze ohne monatliche Grundgebühr". D.h. die Kosten pro Monat variieren abhängig von der Nutzungsintensität. Bei Nicht-Nutzung liegen sie bei 0 - bei starker Nutzung steigen sie beliebig an.
- Volumenpaket = Monatliches Kontingent an Freiminuten zu festem Preis (Euro pauschal), darüber hinaus wird meist nutzungsabhängig abgerechnet. Bspw. "120 Freiminuten in alle Netze für €9 monatliche Gebühr, danach 9 cent pro Minute". D.h. die Kosten pro Monat liegen bei mindestens €9 und können ggf. steigen, wenn die 120 Freiminuten ausgereizt sind.
- Flat-Rate = Unberenztes Telefonieren zu festem Preis (Euro pauschal). Bspw. "Flat-Rate in alle Netze für €40 pro Monat". D.h. egal wie viel telefoniert wird, die Kosten liegen fix bei €40 pro Monat.

Die Daten werden im Rahmen einer Dissertation erhoben und dienen der wissenschaftlichen Forschung. Alle Antworten sind anonym – es gibt keine richtigen oder falschen Antworten. Antworten Sie bitte spontan und ohne langes Überlegen. Die Bearbeitung des Fragebogens dauert ca. 8 Minuten.

Soziodemographische Daten

Bitte nennen Sie uns Ihr Alter: ________
Was ist Ihr Geschlecht? O Männlich O Weiblich

Bitte geben Sie das ungefähres monatliche Bruttoeinkommen Ihres Haushalts an

- unter €1.500
- €1.500 bis €2.499
- €2.500 bis €3.499
- €3.500 bis €4.499
- €4.500 bis €5.499
- €5.500 bis €6.499
- €6.500 bis €7.499
- €7.500 oder mehr

Was ist Ihr höchster Bildungsabschluss?

- Kein Schulabschluss
- Volks- / Hauptschulabschluss
- Mittlere Reife / Realschule
- Abitur oder Fachhochschulreife
- Universitäts- oder Fachholschulabschluss
- Promotion / Habilitation

Haben Sie einen Mobilfunkvertrag?
(Antworten Sie bitte mit nein, wenn Sie eine Pre-Paid Karte nutzen, oder die Rechnung von einer anderen Person/Firma bezahlt wird.)

- Ja
- Nein

Bei welchem Mobilfunkanbieter?

- 1&1
- Base
- Blau
- Deutsche Telekom / T-Mobile
- Deutschland SIM
- Drillisch
- E-Plus
- Fonic
- Lidl
- Mobilcom
- O2
- Phonex
- Prima
- Simyo
- Vodafone
- Andere: ________________

Bitte wählen Sie Ihren Tarif für Sprachtelefonie aus:
(Unabhängig davon, ob SMS oder Datennutzung inkludiert ist)

- Pay-Per-Use: Nutzungsabhängiges Entgelt mit/ohne Grundgebühr (beinhaltet Tarife mit Kostenschutz-/airbag)
- Volumenpaket: Monatliches Kontingent an Freiminuten, danach nutzungsabhängiges Entgelt
- Flat-Rate ins eigene Netz und ins Deutsche Festnetz, nutzungsbasiertes Entgelt für alle anderen Gespräche
- Flat-Rate in alle Deutschen Netze inkl. Festnetz

Geben Sie bitte den Namen Ihres Mobilfunktarifs ein (Falls Sie die genaue Bezeichnung nicht kennen, umschreiben Sie den Tarif bitte oder lassen das Feld leer):

____

Bitte geben Sie grob in Euro Ihre monatlichen Ausgaben für Mobiltelefonie an:
Wie hoch ist Ihre gesamte Mobilfunkrechnung im Durchschnitt:

____

Wie hoch ist die Gebühr für Ihre Flat-Rate / Ihr Volumenpaket für Sprachtelefonie:

____
(0, falls Sie keine Flat-Rate / kein Volumenpaket haben)

Reale Kunden

Wissenschaftliche Untersuchungen haben ergeben, dass einige Kunden Ihre Flat-Rate / Ihr Volumenpaket nicht ausnutzen und im Vergleich zu Pay-Per-Use mehr zahlen...
Ab wieviel Euro Preisersparnis pro Monat durch einen Tarifwechsel zu Pay-Per-Use bei Ihrem Anbieter würden Sie die Vorteile Ihrer Flat-Rate / Ihres Volumenpakets aufgeben und zu Pay-Per-Use wechseln? Gehen Sie davon aus, dass ein Tarifwechsel jederzeit möglich ist und keine zusätzlichen Kosten verursacht. Bitte geben Sie ganz-zahlige Euro Beträge ein.

- Bis zu welcher Preisdifferenz würden Sie noch auf keinen Fall an einen Tarifwechsel denken?

  ____

- Ab welchem Betrag würden Sie anfangen, über einen Tarifwechsel nachzudenken?

  ____

- Bis zu welcher Preisdifferenz wäre das Beibehalten der Flat-Rate gerade noch vorstellbar?

  ____

- Ab welcher Preisdifferenz würden Sie auf jeden Fall den Tarif wechseln?

  ____

Ab wieviel Euro Preisersparnis pro Monat durch einen Wechsel zu Pay-Per-Use bei der Konkurrenz würden Sie Ihren Provider verlassen, die Vorteile Ihrer Flat-Rate / Ihres Volumenpakets aufgeben und zu Pay-Per-Use bei einem günstigeren Anbieter wechseln? Gehen Sie davon aus, dass ein Provider Wechsel zum übernächsten Monat möglich ist, Sie gegen eine geringe Gebühr Ihre Rufnummer behalten können und Ihre Erreichbarkeit am Telefon für maximal einen Tag eingeschränkt ist. Bitte geben Sie ganz-zahlige Euro Beträge ein.

- Bis zu welcher Preisdifferenz würden Sie noch auf keinen Fall an einen Providerwechsel denken?

  ____

- Ab welchem Betrag würden Sie anfangen, über einen Providerwechsel nachzudenken?

  ____

- Bis zu welcher Preisdifferenz wäre das Beibehalten des aktuellen Providers gerade noch vorstellbar?

  ____

- Ab welcher Preisdifferenz würden Sie auf jeden Fall den Provider wechseln?

  ____

Hypothetisches Szenario PrimeTel

Im Folgenden geht es um ein hypothetisches Szenario: Sie sind Kunde von PRIMETEL! Bitte denken Sie bei der Beantwortung aller kommenden Fragen nicht an Ihren eigenen Mobilfunkanbieter, sondern stellen Sie sich vor, Kunde des Mobilfunkanbieters PRIMETEL zu sein: PRIMETEL ist ein Premium Anbieter. D.h. PRIMETEL bietet höchste Sprachqualität und Erreichbarkeit bei 100% Netzabdeckung und bestem Kundenservice. Ihr Tarif bei PRIMETEL ist eine Flat-Rate in alle Deutschen Netze zu einem monatlichen Preis von €80. Egal wie viel Sie Ihr Handy nutzen, Sie zahlen immer €80.

Wissenschaftliche Untersuchungen haben ergeben, dass einige Kunden Ihre Flat-Rate nicht ausnutzen und im Vergleich zu Pay-Per-Use mehr zahlen... Ab wieviel Euro Preisersparnis pro Monat durch einen Tarifwechsel von der Flat-Rate zu Pay-Per-Use innerhalb des Providers PRIMETEL würden Sie die Vorteile der Flat-Rate aufgeben und zu Pay-Per-Use wechseln? Gehen Sie davon aus, dass ein Tarifwechsel jederzeit möglich ist und keine zusätzlichen Kosten verursacht. Bitte geben Sie ganz-zahlige Euro Beträge ein.

- Bis zu welcher Preisdifferenz würden Sie noch auf keinen Fall an einen Tarifwechsel denken?

  ______

- Ab welchem Betrag würden Sie anfangen, über einen Tarifwechsel nachzudenken?

  ______

- Bis zu welcher Preisdifferenz wäre das Beibehalten der Flat-Rate gerade noch vorstellbar?

  ______

- Ab welcher Preisdifferenz würden Sie auf jeden Fall den Tarif wechseln?

  ______

Ab wieviel Euro Preisersparnis pro Monat durch einen Wechsel von der Flat-Rate zu Pay-Per-Use bei der Konkurrenz würden Sie den Provider PRIMETEL verlassen, die Vorteile der Flat-Rate aufgeben und zu Pay-Per-Use bei einem günstigeren Anbieter wechseln? Gehen Sie davon aus, dass ein Provider Wechsel zum übernächsten Monat möglich ist, Sie gegen eine geringe Gebühr Ihre Rufnummer behalten können und Ihre Erreichbarkeit am Telefon für maximal einen Tag eingeschränkt ist. Bitte geben Sie ganz-zahlige Euro Beträge ein.

- Bis zu welcher Preisdifferenz würden Sie noch auf keinen Fall an einen Providerwechsel denken?

  ______

- Ab welchem Betrag würden Sie anfangen, über einen Providerwechsel nachzudenken?

  ______

- Bis zu welcher Preisdifferenz wäre das Beibehalten des aktuellen Providers gerade noch vorstellbar?

  ______

- Ab welcher Preisdifferenz würden Sie auf jeden Fall den Provider wechseln?

  ______

Hypothetisches Szenario GünsTel

Im Folgenden geht es um ein hypothetisches Szenario: Sie sind Kunde von GÜNSTEL! Bitte denken Sie bei der Beantwortung aller kommenden Fragen nicht an Ihren eigenen Mobilfunkanbieter, sondern stellen Sie sich vor, Kunde des Mobilfunkanbieters GÜNSTEL zu sein: GÜNSTEL ist ein low-cost Anbieter. D.h. es gibt keine Ladengeschäft und der Service ist ausschließlich online oder telefonisch zu erreichen. Die Sprachqualität ist ausreichend und Netzabeckung ist in 90% von Deutschland vorhanden. Ihr Tarif bei GÜNSTEL ist eine Flat-Rate in alle Deutschen Netze zu einem monatlichen Preis von €40. Egal wie viel Sie Ihr Handy nutzen, Sie zahlen immer €40.

Wissenschaftliche Untersuchungen haben ergeben, dass einige Kunden Ihre Flat-Rate nicht ausnutzen und im Vergleich zu Pay-Per-Use mehr zahlen... Ab wieviel Euro Preisersparnis pro Monat durch einen Tarifwechsel von der Flat-Rate zu Pay-Per-Use innerhalb des Providers GÜNSTEL würden Sie die Vorteile der Flat-Rate aufgeben und zu Pay-Per-Use wechseln? Gehen Sie davon aus, dass ein Tarifwechsel jederzeit möglich ist und keine zusätzlichen Kosten verursacht. Bitte geben Sie ganz-zahlige Euro Beträge ein.

- Bis zu welcher Preisdifferenz würden Sie noch auf keinen Fall an einen Tarifwechsel denken?

  ____

- Ab welchem Betrag würden Sie anfangen, über einen Tarifwechsel nachzudenken?

  ____

- Bis zu welcher Preisdifferenz wäre das Beibehalten der Flat-Rate gerade noch vorstellbar?

  ____

- Ab welcher Preisdifferenz würden Sie auf jeden Fall den Tarif wechseln?

  ____

Ab wieviel Euro Preisersparnis pro Monat durch einen Wechsel von der Flat-Rate zu Pay-Per-Use bei der Konkurrenz würden Sie den Provider GÜNSTEL verlassen, die Vorteile der Flat-Rate aufgeben und zu Pay-Per-Use bei einem günstigeren Anbieter wechseln? Gehen Sie davon aus, dass ein Provider Wechsel zum übernächsten Monat möglich ist, Sie gegen eine geringe Gebühr Ihre Rufnummer behalten können und Ihre Erreichbarkeit am Telefon für maximal einen Tag eingeschränkt ist. Bitte geben Sie ganz-zahlige Euro Beträge ein.

- Bis zu welcher Preisdifferenz würden Sie noch auf keinen Fall an einen Providerwechsel denken?

  ____

- Ab welchem Betrag würden Sie anfangen, über einen Providerwechsel nachzudenken?

  ____

- Bis zu welcher Preisdifferenz wäre das Beibehalten des aktuellen Providers gerade noch vorstellbar?

  ____

- Ab welcher Preisdifferenz würden Sie auf jeden Fall den Provider wechseln?

  ____

References

Allais, P. M. (1953). Le Comportement de l'Homme Rationnel devant le Risque: Critique des Postulats et Axiomes de l'Ecole Americaine. *Econometrica*, *21*(4), 503-546.

Allison, P. D. (2010). *Survival Analysis Using SAS: A Practical Guide* (Second Edi.). Cary, NC, USA: SAS Publishing.

Andersson, P., & Engelberg, E. (2006). Affective and Rational Consumer Choice Modes: The Role of Intuition, Analytical Decision-Making, and Attitudes to Money.

Bagozzi, R. P., & Baumgartner, H. (1994). The Evaluation of Structural Equation Models and Hypothesis Testing. In R. P. Bagozzi (Ed.), *Principles in Marketing Research* (pp. 386-422). Cambridge.

Bagozzi, R. P., & Yi, Y. (1988). On the Evaluation of Structural Equation Models. *Journal of the Academy of Marketing Science*, *16*(1), 74-94.

Bargh, J. A., & Chartrand, T. L. (2000). Studying the Mind in the Middle: a Practical Guide to Priming and Automaticity Research. In H. T. Reis & C. M. Judd (Eds.), *Handbook of Research Methods in Social and Personality Psychology*. New York: University Press.

Baron, R. M., & Kenny, D. A. (1986). The Moderator-Mediator Variable Distinction in Social Psychological Research: Conceptual, Strategic, and Statistical Considerations. *Journal of Personality and Social Psychology*, *51*(6), 1173-1182.

Batra, R., & Ahtola, O. T. (1991). Measuring the Hedonic and Utilitarian Sources of Consumer Attitudes. *Marketing Letters*, *2*(2), 159-170.

Bearden, W. O., Netemeyer, R. G., & Mobley, M. F. (1993). *Handbook of Marketing Scales: Multi Item Measures for Marketing and Consumer Behavior Research*. Newbury Park.

Berger, P. D., & Nasr, N. I. (1998). Customer Lifetime Value: Marketing Models and Applications. *Journal of Interactive Marketing*, *12*(1), 17-30.

Berry, C. J. (1994). *The Idea of Luxury*. Cambridge, UK: Cambridge University Press.

Biehal, G., Stephens, D., & Curio, E. (1992). Attitude Toward the Ad and Brand Choice. *Journal of Advertising*, *21*(3), 19-36.

Bitner, M. J. (1993). Managing the Evidence of Service. In E. E. Scheuing & W. F. Christopher (Eds.), *The Service Quality Handbook* (pp. 358-370). New York: Amacom Book Division.

Brown, S. J., & Sibley, D. S. (1986). *The Theory of Public Utility Pricing.* Cambridge, UK.: Cambridge University Press.

Burnham, T. a., Frels, J. K., & Mahajan, V. (2003). Consumer Switching Costs: A Typology, Antecedents, and Consequences. *Journal of the Academy of Marketing Science, 31*(2), 109-126.

Carmon, Z., & Simonson, I. (1998). Price-Quality Trade-Offs in Choice versus Matching: New Insights into the Prominence Effect. *Journal of Consumer Psychology, 7*(4), 323-343.

Carroll, J. S. (1978). The Effect of Imagining an Event on Expectations for the Event: An Interpretation in Terms of the Availability Heuristic. *Journal of Experimental Social Psychology, 96*, 88-96.

Carson, R. T., Louviere, J. J., Anderson, D. A., Arabie, P., Bunch, D. S., Hensher, D. A., Johnson, R. M., et al. (1994). Experimental Analysis of Choice. *Marketing Letters, 5*(4), 351-367.

Chitturi, R., Raghunathan, R., & Mahajan, V. (2007). Form Versus Function: How the Intensities of Specific Emotions Evoked in Functional Versus Hedonic Trade-Offs Mediate Product Preferences. *Journal of Marketing Research, 44*(November), 702-714.

Chitturi, R., Raghunathan, R., & Mahajan, V. (2008). Delight by Design: The Role of Hedonic Versus Utilitarian Benefits. *Journal of Marketing, 72*(3), 48-63.

Choi, S.-K., Lee, M.-H., & Chung, G.-H. (2001). Competition in Korean Mobile Telecommunications Market: Business Strategy and Regulatory Environment. *Telecommunications Policy, 25*(1-2), 125-138.

Cureton, E. E., & D'Agostino, R. B. (1983). *Factor Analysis: an Applied Approach.* New York: Hillside.

Dearden, J. (1978). Cost Accounting Comes to Service Industries. *Harvard Business Review, 56*(5), 132-141.

Deliza, R., & MacFie, H. J. H. (1996). The Generation of Sensory Expectation by External Cues and its Effect on Sensory Perception and Hedonic Ratings: a Review. *Journal of Sensory Studies, 11*(2), 103-128.

Della Vigna, S., & Malmendier, U. (2006). Paying Not to Go to the Gym. *American Economic Review*, *96*(3), 694-719.

Desiraju, R., & Shugan, S. M. (1999). Strategic Service Pricing and Yield Management. *Journal of Marketing*, *63*(January), 44-56.

Dess, G. G., & Davis, P. S. (1984). Porter's (1980) Generic Strategies as Determinants of Strategic Group Membership and Organizational Performance. *Academy of Management Journal*, *27*(3), 467-488.

Dhar, R., & Wertenbroch, K. (2000). Consumer Choice Between Hedonic and Utilitarian Goods. *Journal of Marketing Research*, *37*(1), 60-71.

D'Aveni, R. A. (1994). *Hypercompetition. Managing the Dynamics of Strategic Maneuvering. New York.* New York: The Free Press.

Einhorn, H. J., & Hogarth, R. (1986). Decision Making under Ambiguity. *Journal of Business*, *59*(4), 225-250.

Epley, N., Savitsky, K., & Gilovich, T. (2002). Empathy Neglect: Reconciling the Spotlight Effect and the Correspondence Bias. *Journal of Personality and Social Psychology*, *83*(2), 300 -312.

Fornell, C., & Larcker, D. F. (1981). Evaluating Structural Equation Models with Unobservable Variables and Measurement Error. *Journal of Marketing Research*, *18*(2), 39-50.

Gill, T. (2008). Convergent Products: What Functionalities Add More Value to the Base? *Journal of Marketing*, *72*(March), 46-62.

Gourville, J. T., & Soman, D. (1998). Payment Depreciation: the Behavioral Effects of Temporally Separating Payments From Consumption. *Journal of Consumer Research*, *25*(2), 160-174.

Grewal, R., Cote, J. a., & Baumgartner, H. (2004). Multicollinearity and Measurement Error in Structural Equation Models: Implications for Theory Testing. *Marketing Science*, *23*(4), 519-529.

Grönroos, C. (1994). From Marketing Mix to Relationship Marketing: Towards a Paradigm Shift in Marketing. *Management Decision*, *32*(2), 4-20.

Grønnesby, J. K., & Borgan, O. (1996). A Method for Checking Regression Models in Survival Analysis Based on the Risk Score. *Lifetime Data Analysis*, *2*(4), 315-28.

Gupta, S., & Lehmann, D. R. (2003). Customers as Assets. *Journal of Interactive Marketing, 17*(1), 9-24.

Gupta, S., Hanssens, D., Hardie, B., Kahn, W., Kumar, V., Lin, N., Ravishanker, N., et al. (2006). Modeling Customer Lifetime Value. *Journal of Service Research, 9*(2), 139-155.

Hayes, A. F., & Preacher, K. J. (2011). Indirect and Direct Effects of a Multicategorical Causal Agent in Statistical Mediation Analysis.

Heath, C., & Soll, J. B. (1996). Mental Budgeting and Consumer Decisions. *Journal of Consumer Research, 23*(1), 40-52.

Heidenreich, S., & Handrich, M. (2010). The Fascination of Limitless Consumption – An Empirical Study of Existence and Causes of Flat-Rate Biases in the Cellular Mobile Industry. *Global Marketing Conference* (pp. 1-6). Tokyo, Japan.

Hightower, R., Brady, M. K., & Baker, T. L. (2002). Investigating the Role of the Physical Environment in Hedonic Service Consumption: an Exploratory Study of Sporting Events. *Journal of Business Research, 55*, 697-707.

Hill, C. W. L. (1988). Differentiation Versus Low Cost or Differentiation and Low Cost: A Contingency Framework. *Academy of Management Review, 13*(3), 401-412.

Hill, D. J., Blodgett, J., Baer, R., & Wakefield, K. (2004). An Investigation of Visualization and Documentation Strategies in Services Advertising. *Journal of Service Research, 7*(2), 155-166.

Hobson, M., & Spady, R. (1988). The Demand for Local Telephone Service Under Optional Local Measured Service. *Bellcore Economics Discussion Paper, 50.*

Hosmer, David W., Lemeshow, S., & May, S. (2008). *Applied Survival Analysis: Regression Modeling of Time-to-Event Data* (Second Edi.). Hoboken, NJ, USA: John Wiley & Sons.

Howell, B. (2010). Flat-Rate Tariffs and Competitive Entry in Telecommunications Markets.

Hsee, C. K., & Rottenstreich, Y. (2004). Music, Pandas, and Muggers: on the Affective Psychology of Value. *Journal of Experimental Psychology: General, 133*(1), 23-30.

Iyengar, R., Ansari, A., & Gupta, S. (2007). A Model of Consumer Learning for Service Quality and Usage. *Journal of Marketing Research*, *44*(4), 529-544.

Johansson-Stenman, O., Carlsson, F., & Daruvala, D. (2002). Measuring Future Grandparents' Preferences for Equality and Relative Standing. *The Economic Journal*, *112*(479), 362-383.

Joo, Y.-H., Jun, J.-K., & Kim, B.-D. (2002). Encouraging Customers to Pay Less for Mobile Telecommunication Services. *Journal of Database Marketing*, *9*(4), 350-359.

Kahneman, D., & Frederick, S. (2002). Representativeness Revisited: Attribute Substitution in Intuitive Judgment. In T. Gilovich, D. Griffin, & D. Kahneman (Eds.), *Heuristics and Biases: The Psychology of Intuitive Judgment* (pp. 49-81). Cambridge: Cambridge University Press.

Kahneman, D., & Tversky, A. (1979). Prospect Theory: An Analysis of Decision under Risk. *Econometrica*, *47*(2), 263-292.

Kahneman, D., Ritov, I., & Schkade, D. (2000). Economic Preferences or Attitude Expressions? An Analysis of Dollar Responses to Public Issues. In D. Kahneman & A. Tversky (Eds.), *Choices, Values, and Frames* (pp. 642-672). New York: Cambridge University Press.

Khan, U., Dhar, R., & Wertenbroch, K. (2004). A Behavioral Theoretic Perspective on Hedonic and Utilitarian Choice. In S. Ratneshwar & D. G. Mick (Eds.), *Inside Consumption: Frontiers of Research on Consumer Motives, Goals, and Desires* (pp. 144-165). New York: Routledge.

Kivetz, R. (1999). Advances in Research on Mental Accounting and Reason-Based Choice. *Marketing Letters*, *10*(August), 249-266.

Kivetz, R., & Simonson, I. (2002). Earning the Right to Indulge: Effort as a Determinant of Customer Preferences Toward Frequency Program Rewards. *Journal of Marketing Research*, *39*(2), 155-170.

Kling, J. P., & van Der Ploeg, S. S. (1990). Estimating Local Elasticities with a Model of Stochastic Class of Service and Usage Choice. In A. de Fontenay, M. H. Shugard, & D. S. Sibley (Eds.), *Telecommunications Demand Modelling. An Integrated View*. Amsterdam.

Kolb, B., & Whishaw, Q. (2003). *Fundamentals of Human Neuropsychology* (5th ed., p. 763). Worth Publishers, Inc.

Kridel, D. J., Lehman, D. E., & Weisman, D. L. (1993). Option Value, Telecommunications Demand, and Policy. *Information Economics and Policy*, *5*(2), 125-144.

Krieger, A. M., & Green, P. E. (1991). Designing Pareto Optimal Stimuli for Multiattribute Choice Experiments. *Marketing Letters*, *2*(4), 337-348.

Lambrecht, A., & Skiera, B. (2006). Paying Too Much and Being Happy About It: Existence, Causes, and Consequences of Tariff-Choice Biases. *Journal of Marketing Research*, *43*(2), 212-223.

Lambrecht, A., Seim, K., & Skiera, B. (2005). Does Uncertainty Matter? Consumer Behavior under Three-Part Tariffs.

Levin, I. P., & Gaeth, G. J. (1988). How Consumers are Affected by the Framing of Attribute Information Before and After Consuming the Product. *Journal of Consumer Research*, *15*(3), 374.

Li, S. (1995). Survival Analysis. *Marketing Research*, *7*(4), 17-23.

Loewenstein, G. (2001). The Creative Destruction of Decision Research. *Journal of Consumer Research*, *28*(3), 499-505.

Lu, J. (2002). Predicting Customer Churn in the Telecommunications Industry — An Application of Survival Analysis Modeling Using SAS. *SAS User Group International Online Proceedings*, *114-27*.

Maslow, A. H. (1968). *Toward a Psychology of Being* (Second Edi.). Princeton, NJ.

May, S, & Hosmer, D. W. (1998). A Simplified Method of Calculating an Overall Goodness-of-Fit Test for the Cox Proportional Hazards Model. *Lifetime data analysis*, *4*(2), 109-20.

Mehta, N., Rajiv, S., & Srinivasan, K. (2003). Price Uncertainty and Consumer Search: A Structural Model of Consideration Set Formation. *Marketing Science*, *22*(1), 58-84.

Menard, S. W. (2002). *Longitudinal Research* (2nd ed.). Thousand Oaks, CA, USA: Sage Publications, Inc.

Miller, K. M., Hofstetter, R., Krohmer, H., & Zhang, Z. J. (2011). How Should Consumers' Willingness to Pay Be Measured? An Empirical Comparison of State-of-the-Art Approaches. *Journal of Marketing Research*, *48*(February), 172 -184.

Miravete, E. J. (2000). Estimating Demand For Local Telephone Service with Asymmetric Information and Optional Calling Plans. *Economic Policy*.

Miravete, E. J. (2002). Choosing the Wrong Calling Plan? Ignorance and Learning. *American Economic Review*, *93*(1), 297-310.

Mitchell, B. M., & Vogelsang, I. (1991). *Telecommunications Pricing: Theory and Practice* (1st ed.). Cambridge: Cambridge University Press.

Morgan, R. M., & Hunt, S. D. (1994). The Commitment-Trust Theory of Relationship Marketing. *Journal of Marketing*, *58*(3), 20-38.

Murray, A. I. (1988). A Contingency View of Porter's "Generic Strategies." *The Academy of Management Review*, *13*(3), 390.

Nunes, J. C. (2000). A Cognitive Model of People's Usage Estimations. *Journal of Marketing Research*, *37*, 397-409.

Nunnally, J. C. (1978). *Psychometric Theory* (Second Edi.). New York.

Okada, E. M. (2005). Justification Effects on Consumer Choice of Hedonic and Utilitarian Goods. *Journal of Marketing Research*, *42*(1), 43-53.

O'Brien, R. M. (2007). A Caution Regarding Rules of Thumb for Variance Inflation Factors. *Quality and Quantity*, *41*(5), 673-690.

O'Curry, S., & Strahilevitz, M. (2001). Probability and Mode of Acquisition Effects on Choices Between Hedonic and Utilitarian Options. *Marketing Letters*, *12*, 37-49.

Perdue, B. C., & Sommers, J. O. (1986). Checking the Success of Manipulations in Marketing Experiments. *Journal of Marketing Research*, *23*(4), 317-326.

Peterson, C., Semmel, A., Baeyer, C. von, & Abramson, L. (1982). The Attributional Style Questionnaire. *Cognitive Therapy and Research*, *6*(3), 287-299.

Pigou, A. C. (1920). *The Economics of Welfare*. London: Macmillan.

Porter, M. E. (1980). *Competitive Strategy*. New York: Free Press.

Porter, M. E. (1985). *Competitive Advantage: Creating and Sustaining Superior Performance*. New York: Free Press.

Preacher, K. J., & Hayes, A. F. (2008). Asymptotic and Resampling Strategies for Assessing and Comparing Indirect Effects in Multiple Mediator Models. *Behavior Research Methods*, *40*(3), 879-891.

Prelec, D., & Loewenstein, G. (1998). The Red and the Black: Mental Accounting of Savings and Debt. *Marketing Science*, *17*(1), 4-28.

Pugh, S. D. (2001). Service With a Smile: Emotional Contagion in the Service Encounter. *Academy of Management Journal*, *44*(5), 1018-1027.

Reichheld, F. F., & Sasser, W. E. (1990). Zero Defections: Quality Comes to Services. *Harvard Business Review*, *68*(1), 106-107.

Reinartz, W. J., & Kumar, V. (2000). Customer Lifetime Duration: An Empirical Framework for Measurement and Explanation. *Working Paper*.

Riess, M., Rosenfeld, P., Melburg, V., & Tedeschi, J. T. (1981). Self-Serving Attributions: Biased Private Perceptions and Distorted Public Descriptions. *Journal of Personality and Social Psychology*, *41*(2), 224-231.

Santonen, T. (2007). Price Sensitivity as an Indicator of Customer Defection in Retail Banking. *International Journal of Bank Marketing*, *25*(1), 39-55.

Shefrin, H. M., & Thaler, R. (1992). Mental Accounting, Saving, and Self-Control. In G. F. Loewenstein & J. Elster (Eds.), *Choice over Time*. New York.

Shiv, B., Carmon, Z., & Ariely, D. (2005). Placebo Effects of Marketing Actions: Consumers May Get What They Pay For. *Journal of Marketing Research*, *42*(4), 383-393.

Simonson, I., Carmon, Z., Dhar, R., Drolet, A., & Nowlis, S. M. (2001). Consumer Research: in Search of Identity. *Annual Review of Psychology*, *52*, 249-75.

Smith, G. E., Venkatraman, M. P., & Dholakia, R. R. (1999). Diagnosing the Search Cost Effect: Waiting Time and the Moderating Impact of Prior Category Knowledge. *Journal of Economic Psychology*, *20*(3), 285-314.

Statistisches Bundesamt. (2006). Wirtschaftsrechnungen. Einkommens- und Verbrauchsstichprobe, Einkommensverteilung in Deutschland. Wiesbaden: Statistisches Bundesamt.

Statistisches Bundesamt. (2009). Verdienste und Arbeitskosten. Aufschlüsselung der Wirtschaftszweige (WZ) 2008. *DESTATIS*. Wiesbaden: Statistisches Bundesamt.

Strahilevitz, M., & Myers, J. G. (1998). Donations to Charty as Purchase Incentives: How Well They Work May Depend on What You Are Trying to Sell. *Journal of Consumer Research*, *24*(4), 434-446.

Swalm, R. O. (1966). Utility Theory - Insights into Risk Taking. *Harvard Business Review*, *44*(6), 123-136.

Thaler, R. (1985). Mental Accounting and Consumer Choice. *Marketing Science*, *4*(3), 199-214.

Thomas, D. K. E. (1978). Strategy is Different in Service Businesses. *Harvard Business Review*, *56*(4), 158-166.

Train, K. E. (1991). *Optimal Regulation. The Economic Theory of Natural Monopoly*. Cambridge (MA): MIT Press.

Train, K. E., Ben-Akiva, M., & Atherton, T. (1989). Consumption Patterns and Self-Selecting Tariffs. *The Review of Economics and Statistics*, *71*(1), 62-73.

Train, K. E., McFadden, D. L., & Ben-Akiva, M. (1987). The Demand for Local Telephone Service: a Fully Discrete Model of Residential Calling Patterns and Service Choices. *Rand Journal of Economics*, *18*(1), 109-123.

Tversky, A., & Kahneman, D. (1973). Availability: A Heuristic for Judging Frequency and Probability. *Cognitive Psychology*, *5*, 207-232.

Tversky, A., & Kahneman, D. (1991). Loss Aversion in Riskless Choice: A Reference-Dependent Model. *Quarterly Journal of Economics*, *106*(4), 1039-1061.

Uhrich, F., Sandner, U., Resatsch, F., Leimeister, J. M., & Krcmar, H. (2008). RFID in Retailing and Customer Relationship Management. *The Communications of the Association for Information Systems*, *23*(13), 219-234.

Vargo, S. L., & Akaka, M. A. (2009). Service-Dominant Logic as a Foundation for Service Science: Clarifications. *Science*, *1*(1), 32-41.

Vargo, S. L., & Lusch, R. F. (2004). Evolving to a New Dominant Logic for Marketing. *Journal of Marketing*, *68*(1), 1-17.

Viellechner, O. (2010). *Incumbent Inertia in Light of Disruptive Change in the Airline Industry: Causal Factors and Top Management Moderators* (First Edit.). Stuttgart: Ibidem.

Voss, K. E., Spangenberg, E. R., & Grohmann, B. (2003). Measuring the Hedonic and Utilitarian Dimensions of Consumer Attitude. *Journal of Marketing Research*, *40*(3), 310-320.

Wakefield, K. L., & Inman, J. J. (2003). Situational Price Sensitivity: the Role of Consumption Occasion, Social Context and Income. *Journal of Retailing*, *79*(4), 199-212.

Wangenheim, F. von. (2005). Postswitching Negative Word of Mouth. *Journal of Service Research*, *8*(1), 67-78.

Wertenbroch, K. (1998). Consumption Self-Control by Rationing Purchase Quantities of Virtue and Vice. *Marketing Science*, *17*(4), 317-337.

Westendorp, P. van. (1976). NSS-Price Sensitivity Meter: A New Approach to Study Consumer Perception of Prices. *Venice ESOMAR Congress* (pp. 139-167). Amsterdam: European Marketing Research Society.

Winer, R. S. (2005). *Pricing*. Cambridge, MA.

Wolfe, M. (1955). The Concept of Economic Sectors. *The Quarterly Journal of Economics*, *69*(3), 402-420.

Wong, K. K.-K. (2010a). Fighting Churn with Rate Plan Right-Sizing: a Customer Retention Strategy for the Wireless Telecommunications Industry. *The Service Industries Journal*, *30*(13), 2261-2271.

Wong, K. K.-K. (2010b). Should Wireless Carriers Protect Residential Voice Subscribers from High Overage and Underage Charges? Insights from the Canadian Telecommunications Market. *Telecommunications Policy*, *34*(8), 461-481.

Zeithaml, V. A., Parasuraman, A., & Berry, L. L. (2010). Problems and Services Strategies in Marketing. *Journal of Marketing*, *49*(2), 33-46.

Zhao, X., Lynch Jr., J. G., & Chen, Q. (2010). Reconsidering Baron and Kenny: Myths and Truths about Mediation Analysis. *Journal of Consumer Research*, *37*(2), 197-206.

Zomerdijk, L. G., & Voss, C. A. (2009). Service Design for Experience-Centric Services. *Journal of Service Research*, *13*(1), 67-82.

***ibidem*-Verlag**

Melchiorstr. 15

D-70439 Stuttgart

info@ibidem-verlag.de

www.ibidem-verlag.de
www.ibidem.eu
www.edition-noema.de
www.autorenbetreuung.de

www.ingramcontent.com/pod-product-compliance
Lightning Source LLC
Chambersburg PA
CBHW080551220326
41599CB00032B/6444

* 9 7 8 3 8 3 8 2 0 4 7 9 6 *